RENEWAL AND THE
POWERS OF DARKNESS

By the same author, also published by Servant

Ecumenism and Charismatic Renewal:
Theological and Pastoral Orientations

Charismatic Renewal and Social Action:
A Dialogue (with Helder Camara)

A New Pentecost?

Essays on Renewal

Renewal and the Powers of Darkness

Cardinal Léon-Joseph Suenens

Foreword by
Cardinal Joseph Ratzinger

Malines Document IV

SERVANT BOOKS
Ann Arbor, Michigan

2 0 6 2 11

Published in the United States by Servant Books
                                    P.O. Box 8617
                                    Ann Arbor, Michigan 48107

ISBN 0-89283-125-1

83 84 85 10 9 8 7 6 5 4 3 2 1

Printed in the United States of America

CONTENTS

Part Two: Charismatic Renewal and 'The Powers of Darkness'

VI: The Charismatic Renewal As 'Experience' of the Holy Spirit

VII: The Renewal and a Deeper Sense of Evil

VIII: The Renewal and the Demonology Underlying the Practice of Deliverance

IX: The Practice of 'Deliverance' in Catholic Circles

X: The Renewal and the Casting Out of Demons: Theological Observations

Foreword

ALTHOUGH THE POSTCONCILIAR PERIOD hardly appears to fulfill the hope of Pope John XXIII when he prayed for 'a New Pentecost,' his prayer did not remain wholly unanswered.

At the heart of a world imbued with a rationalist scepticism, a new experience of the Holy Spirit suddenly burst forth. And, since then, that experience has assumed the breadth of a worldwide Renewal movement.

What the New Testament tells us about the charisms—which were seen as visible signs of the coming of the Spirit—is not just ancient history, over and done with, for it is once again becoming extremely topical. But in those very places where the Spirit of God is coming closer to us, we are also witnessing, in contrast, the awakening of a keener awareness of what sets itself against him. Chesterton already emphasized this point in his well-known phrase: 'A saint is someone who knows that he is a sinner.'

While a rationalist and reductionist theology is explaining away the Devil and the world of evil spirits as a mere label for everything that threatens man in his subjectivity, a new, concrete awareness of the Powers of Evil and their cunning, which threaten man, is growing in the context of the Renewal.

This awareness has given rise to a 'prayer of deliverance from the Devil' which has developed to the point of resembling a rite of exorcism and of becoming, today, an integral part of the life of some charismatic groups.

It is more than obvious that this practice lays itself open to considerable dangers which cannot be brushed aside with a facile irony, any more than they can be dismissed through a superficial and more or less rationalist type of critique.

Only a genuine highway code, elaborated from within and

rooted in the very area of the Spirit's gifts can meet the need for discernment in this matter. And these gifts include wisdom and moderation, which are both inspired by the Spirit and comply with St Paul's plea: 'Do not quench the Spirit . . . but test everything and hold on to what is good' (1 Thess. 5:19, 21).

In the book I have the pleasure of presenting, Cardinal Suenens has undertaken the task of applying that discernment of spirits and of outlining a conduct inspired by the Spirit. For this we are much indebted to him. His work is as important for the Renewal movement as for the whole Church.

First he raises the basic question which is decisive for the fruitful growth of the Renewal: What is the relation between personal experience and the common faith of the Church? Both factors are important: a dogmatic faith unsupported by personal experience remains empty; mere personal experience unrelated to the faith of the Church remains blind.

The isolation of experience constitutes a serious threat to true Christianity—a threat extending far beyond the Renewal movement. Even if this isolation has a 'pneumatic' origin, it is the price that has to be paid for the empiricism that dominates our time.

Such an isolation of experience is closely linked with the Fundamentalism that separates the Bible from the whole of salvation history and reduces it to an experience of self with no mediation whatsoever. It does justice neither to historical reality, nor to the breadth of the mystery of God. Here, too, the true answer lies in a comprehension of the Bible, in union with the whole Church, and not merely in an isolated historicist reading.

All this shows once again that charism and institution overlap, and that what matters is not the 'we' of the group but the great 'we' of the Church of all times, which alone can provide the adequate and necessary framework, enabling us both to 'hold on to what is good' and to 'discern spirits.'

It is by starting from these basic categories of the spiritual life that Cardinal Suenens restores the question of the devils to its true dimension and situates the prayer of deliverance.

Thus the mystery of iniquity fits into the fundamental Christian perspective; that is to say, the perspective of Jesus Christ's Resurrection and victory over the Powers of Evil. In this light, the Christian's freedom and calm assurance that 'casts out fear' (1 John 4:18) take on their full dimension: truth excludes fear and, by that very fact, enables the Christian to recognize the power of the Evil One.

Ambiguity is a distinctive feature of the demonic phenomenon: consequently, the mainspring of the Christian's fight against the Devil is his ability to live day after day in the light of faith.

I strongly advise Christians to read and study this book attentively, so that from the fundamental perspectives opened up by Cardinal Suenens they may grasp the practical directives that ensue for the use of the Renewal groups and especially for the practice of the prayer of deliverance.

I also urge them to pay special attention to the Cardinal's double plea, which deserves the greatest consideration: on the one hand, his appeal to those responsible for the ecclesial ministry—from parish priests to bishops—not to let the Renewal pass them by but to welcome it fully; and on the other, his appeal to the members of the Renewal to cherish and maintain their link with the whole Church and with the charisms of her pastors.

As Prefect of the Congregation for the Doctrine of the Faith, I warmly welcome this work by Cardinal Suenens: it is an important contribution to the blossoming of the spiritual life in today's Church.

I hope that his book will meet with a thoughtful reception both within the Renewal and outside it, and that it will be accepted as the safety-line in exploring the questions he discusses in the following pages.

+ CARDINAL RATZINGER
Rome, Feast of St James, 1982

Preface

THIS FOURTH MALINES DOCUMENT examines a particularly delicate subject. It attempts to answer the question: in theory and in practice, what should be the Christian attitude towards the reality and the influence of the Spirit of Evil in the world?

This is a difficult problem since, by definition, we are dealing with a tenebrous realm to which no approach, whether fundamentalist or rationalist, can afford to be simplistic.

My aim is not to explore the problem in all possible directions, but to explain, more particularly, the Church's view and pastoral practice on the subject, and to compare the mind of the Church with certain beliefs and practices regarding deliverance and exorcism which are observable in Charismatic Renewal groups or communities.

Paul VI very explicitly urged the world to give serious thought to the question of the Evil One's action, which seems so alien to our contemporary outlook. The present study is done in this perspective.

In strict logic, the 'charism of healing,' reactualized by and in the Renewal, should have been studied first; for healing and exorcism are indeed closely related, though by no means identical. But the subject would have proved too vast, and the necessity of clarifying certain points obliges me to choose the most urgent and to give them priority.

My aim is to chart a safe course between two dangers:
—that of underestimating the presence of the Spirit of Evil in the world;
—and that of fighting against the Spirit of Evil without the indispensable discernment and safeguards of the Church.

There is no denying that the Church is faced with a serious pastoral problem which bears on her very mission in the world.

She cannot evade this problem, despite its complexity and delicacy, for what is at stake is her fidelity to the Gospel and her duty to come to grips with the Power of Evil in the contemporary world.

The very fact of writing 'Evil' with a capital shows that, from the outset, I have to make a choice. Should I write the word with a small 'e,' thereby designating, in the broadest sense, the harmful and destructive human influences besetting the individual and society today? Or should I recognize that, in addition to those malign and obscure interhuman forces, there is a Power of Evil, endowed with intelligence and will, at work in the world?

This question and the dilemma it presents cannot be evaded. Either we affirm the Devil's existence, at the risk of seeming out of step with the modern critical outlook, or we dismiss it . . . and then we risk being at variance with the Gospel and the Church's Tradition.

In the following pages my aim is to help steer a safe course between Scylla and Charybdis without underestimating the difficulties. I have not only to affirm with certainty the existence of the Spirit of Evil, but at the same time to warn against the imprudence of venturing into an area beset with pitfalls.

Road safety is ensured by red and green traffic lights, while the intermediate amber light signifies preparedness. Here I would like to offer a similar service.

This *Malines Document IV* confronts a problem which transcends the frontiers of the Charismatic Renewal and concerns us all: it aims to stress the authentic teaching of the Magisterium and to point out certain deviations concerning the practice of deliverance. To facilitate group study and discussion during seminars or meetings, the text has been divided into numbered passages.

Each chapter ends with a prayer taken from the Church's liturgy, and each of these prayers is an invitation to read these pages and to pray them, too, in profound communion with the faith of the Church, which gives our own faith its fullness, vigour and security. The praying Church is already, by that very fact, the teaching Church.

I have written these pages in prayer and suffering, knowing that, on the one hand, they will seem outdated to those who regard the Devil as a myth, and on the other, they will seem insufficiently supported by pastoral experience to those who practice deliverance on a wide scale and fear, moreover, that cautionary advice might discredit the Renewal. I believe, on the contrary, that by clarifying our terms we can only increase the credibility and the immense spiritual potential of the Renewal.

As for experience, I shall simply say that, for my part, I do not doubt that in certain specific cases a demonic influence is at work, and that I have observed, or have been instrumental in, liberating exorcisms. Let me add that I am indebted to the leaders of the Renewal—priests and laymen alike—who, in various parts of the world, have enabled me to ascertain on the spot how deliverance is practiced in their group.

May these pages help to remove obstacles and to make straight the paths of the Lord. More than ever, we all need the enlightenment of the Holy Spirit: he alone can bring us to the understanding of the mystery of the Redemption and to the fullness of Truth. And Truth is already *per se* liberation and deliverance, for as the Lord tells us, 'The truth will make you free.'

May Mary obtain for us from the Lord the grace of entering with humility and spiritual readiness into the discernment and maternal wisdom of the Church!

May she help each one of us to be wholly open to the Holy Spirit and to come to grips, courageously and discerningly, with everything that hinders and opposes God's Reign in this world, our world which, in Paul VI's phrase, is 'both magnificent and painfully tragic.'

+ L.J. Cardinal Suenens

Part One

The Church
and 'The Powers of Darkness'

I

The Devil—Myth or Reality?

1. The faith of the Church

1. We have to admit that today Christians feel a certain unease about pronouncing on the existence of the Devil or devils. Is Satan a myth or a reality? Ought he to be dismissed as a mere fantasy? Is he no more than the symbolic personification of Evil, a hangover from a distant pre-scientific age?

Many Christians opt for the myth, while those who do accept the reality of the Devil feel inhibited and embarrassed when it comes to speaking of him, fearing that they may appear to endorse the popular imagery which surrounds him and to disregard the advances of science.

Catechesis, preaching and the theological lectures given in our universities and seminaries usually avoid the subject. And even in circles where the Devil's existence is discussed, the question of his action and influence in the world is seldom approached. The Devil has managed to pass himself off as an anachronism: this is his greatest act of cunning.

In these circumstances, the modern Christian needs courage to brave the facile sarcasm and the pitying smiles of his contemporaries.

And all the more so as recognizing the Devil's existence hardly squares with what Leo Moulin calls 'the Pelagian optimism of our time.'

So, more than ever, the Christian needs to trust the Church, to let himself be guided by her, to reaffirm from the heart the humble prayer which she places on our lips each time we celebrate the Eucharist:

'Lord, look not on our sins but on the faith of your Church.'

Our personal faith, our poor and wavering faith, finds strength and nourishment in the ecclesial faith that carries it, supports it, and gives it bouyancy and confidence. This is especially true of our faith when confronted with Evil.

2. It is in this filial spirit that we must hear the counsel of Pope Paul VI, who urged us to overcome our unease, to break our silence and to recognize that, even today, the presence of the Evil One is not, alas, an anachronism. Here is a key passage from his declaration:

A living, perverted spiritual being

Evil is not merely a lack of something, but an effective agent, a living, spiritual being, perverted and perverting. A terrible reality. Mysterious and frightening. It is contrary to the teaching of the Bible and the Church to refuse to recognize the existence of such a reality . . . , or to explain it as a pseudo-reality, a conceptual and fanciful personification of the unknown causes of our misfortunes. The Devil was 'a murderer from the beginning . . . and the father of lies,' as Christ defines him (John 8:44-45); he launches sophistic attacks on the moral equilibrium of man . . . Not that every sin is directly attributable to diabolical action; but it is true that those who do not watch over themselves with a certain moral strictness (cf. Matt. 12:45; Eph. 6:11) are exposed to the influence of the 'mysterium iniquitatis' to which St Paul refers (2 Thess. 2:3-12) and run the risk of being damned. [1]

3. And, on the same subject, here are the conclusions of an authorized study, published in the *Osservatore Romano* under the title 'Christian Faith and Demonology' and recommended by the Congregation for the Doctrine of the Faith as a sound basis for the reaffirmation of the Magisterium's doctrine on our theme. The author begins by explaining why Satan's existence has never been the object of a dogmatic declaration:

A constant and lived faith

The Church's position in regard to demonology is clear and firm. It is true that in the course of the centuries the existence of Satan and of the devils has never in fact been the object of an explicit declaration of her Magisterium. The reason for this is that the question was never posed in these terms. Both heretics and the faithful, basing their respective positions on sacred Scripture, were in agreement in recognizing the existence of Satan and the devils and their main misdeeds. This is why, when the reality of the devil is called in question today, it is to the constant and universal belief of the Church and to its main source, the teaching of Christ, that one must appeal, as has been stated. It is in fact in the teaching of the Gospel and as something at the heart of the faith that the existence of the demonic world is shown to be a dogmatic datum. [2]

Then, adducing the teaching of Paul VI, the author shows that he is not making a casual assertion which can be brushed aside and is hardly relevant to the values involved in the mystery of the Redemption:

The present-day unease which we described at the beginning (of our article) does not therefore call into question a secondary element of Christian thinking: it is a question rather of the constant belief of the Church, of her manner of conceiving redemption and, at the root source, of the very consciousness of Jesus. This is why, when His Holiness Pope Paul VI spoke recently of this 'terrible mysterious and frightening reality' of Evil, he could assert with authority: 'he who refuses to recognize its existence . . . departs from the integrity of biblical and ecclesiastical teaching.' Neither exegetes nor theologians can neglect this caution. [3]

Affirming the existence of the Devil, says the author, does not mean drifting into Manichaeism or diminishing our human responsibility and freedom:

Man's responsibility and freedom

4. Let us therefore repeat that by underlining today the existence of demonic reality, the Church intends neither to take us back to the dualistic and Manichaean speculations of former times, nor to propose some rationally acceptable substitute for them. She wishes only to remain faithful to the Gospel and its demands. It is clear that she has never allowed man to rid himself of his responsibility by attributing his faults to the devil. The Church did not hesitate to oppose such escapism when the latter manifested itself, saying with Saint John Chrysostom: 'It is not the devil but men's own carelessness which causes all their falls and all the ills of which they complain.'

For this reason, Christian teaching makes no concession in vigorously defending the freedom and the greatness of man and in emphasizing the omnipotence and goodness of the Creator. It has condemned in the past and will always condemn the too easy use of temptation by the devil as an excuse. It has forbidden superstition just as much as magic. It refused to capitulate doctrinally in the face of fatalism or to diminish freedom in the face of pressure. [4]

Prudence and a keen critical sense are more than ever essential in a domain where discernment itself is difficult and needs guidance:

Necessity of a critical assessment

What is more, when a possible demonic intervention is suggested, the Church always imposes a critical assessment of the evidence, as in the case of miracles. Reserve and prudence are in fact demanded. It is easy to fall victim to imagination and to allow oneself to be led astray by inaccurate accounts distorted in their transmission and incorrectly interpreted. In these cases, therefore, as elsewhere, one must exercise discernment. And one must leave room for research and its findings.[5]

2. Satan, God's opponent?

5. The above allusion to dualistic and Manichaean speculations cautions us against all theories that present the Devil as a kind of Counter-Power, an Antagonist directly opposed to God, vying with him as an equal opponent in a battle.

For we must take care not to envisage Satan as an Antigod, thus making God and the Devil two contending absolutes: the Principle of Good grappling with the Principle of Evil. God is the one and only Absolute, sovereign and transcendent; whereas the Devil, a creature of God and originally good in his ontological reality, plays in Creation the role of a destructive, negative and subordinate parasite. He is the father of lies, of perversion. He is a conscious force who knows, wills, and pursues a destructive goal; thus he lives and works in the Anti-Reign, that is to say, in opposition to the Messianic Kingdom.

Satan must never be regarded as the Adversary who confronts God, defies him and holds him in check.

When, in the first pages of the Bible, Satan, the principle of evil, appears under the guise of a 'serpent,' the sacred text underlines that he is a creature of God (Gen. 3:1). But, above all, he is the enemy of man (Wisd. 2:24), the enemy of God's plan for man. In the *Spiritual Exercises,* St Ignatius calls him 'the enemy of human nature.'

And this is precisely how he is depicted in the first chapters of the Book of Job. In order to tempt man to evil, Satan takes his place among the 'Sons of God who come to attend on the Lord' (Job 1:1, 2, 6).

The reason why the Old Testament is discreet about the role of Satan is, perhaps, that it wishes to prevent Israel from making him a second God. He assumes more importance in the Judaism of Jesus' lifetime, when that danger no longer exists for

Israel, because the time has come for God's absolute transcendence to be fully revealed.

Under the name of Satan (the Adversary) or the Devil (the Calumniator), the Bible presents him as a personal being, invisible in himself, incorporeal, but endowed with knowledge and freedom.

As for the devils, the Greek pagan world identified them with the spirits of the dead or with certain pagan divinities. In the Bible, on the other hand, they designate various 'spirits of evil' whom the New Testament calls 'unclean spirits.'

3. Jesus and the Devil

6. One cannot read the Gospel without being struck by the ubiquity of the Evil One who sets himself against Jesus. The clash of wills is constant, even when it is not a prominent feature of the narrative. No sooner does the Saviour begin his public life than Satan plainly reveals his hostility. The story of Jesus' temptation in the wilderness is, as it were, the preface to the mission that the Saviour is about to fulfill and the key to the drama soon to be enacted on Calvary.

This inevitable confrontation is not just one episode among others, but an anticipation of the final drama, a lifting of the veil that already gives us a glimpse of the mystery of Good Friday. St Luke, moreover, ends his account of the temptation in the wilderness with the words: 'Having exhausted all these ways of tempting him, the devil left him, to return at the appointed time' (Luke 4:13). Doubtless this is an allusion to the ultimate confrontation and Jesus' definitive triumph at the hour of the Passion.

The reference to 'darkness' is repeated in the Gospel so that, reading between the lines, we may apprehend the Enemy's cunning hostility.

When Judas leaves the upper room, 'Satan having entered him,' St John notes that 'night had fallen.' This is not a minor detail, inserted merely for the sake of historical accuracy.

The hostile presence of the Adversary is implicit at every

stage of the narrative, and when Jesus yields up his spirit on the cross, the inspired writer notes—not as a point of detail, but because of the event's deep theological implications—that the sky 'grows dark' over Jerusalem.

Moreover, we find Jesus doing battle with the Tempter throughout his life. Frequently, he admonishes those whom the Devil uses as instruments to tempt him away from the Father's path: the Jews of his time and, on occasion, the Apostles themselves, as in the case of Peter (Matt. 16:23), or again James and John (Luke 9:54-55).

This confrontation with the Evil One is such a constant feature of Jesus' life that we are not entitled to gloss over it or to disregard it.

Notes

1. Paul VI, General Audience of 15 Nov. 1972. Full text in *Osservatore Romano* 23, Nov. 1972, p. 3.
2. Acts of the Holy See, *Christian Faith and Demonology*. Full text in *Osservatore Romano* 10, July 1975, pp. 6-10.
3. Ibid., p. 9.
4. Ibid.
5. Ibid.

Prayer

Let us ask with the faith of the Church to enter fully into the mystery of the Redemption:

FATHER, IN YOUR PLAN OF SALVATION YOUR SON JESUS CHRIST ACCEPTED THE CROSS AND FREED US FROM THE POWER OF THE ENEMY. MAY WE COME TO SHARE THE GLORY OF HIS RESURRECTION.

Prayer for Wednesday of Holy Week

+   +   +

Questions for Reflection and Discussion

1. Recognizing the existence of evil (small 'e') is one thing; recognizing the existence of Evil (capital 'E') is another. In this light, analyse the words of Pope Paul VI (no. 2).

2. Bring out the essential points made in the Document published by the *Osservatore Romano*: why has the existence of Satan never been the object of an explicit declaration of the Magisterium? (no. 3).

3. What exaggerations must be avoided concerning the nature and role of the Devil? (nos. 4 and 5).

4. Note in the Gospel and the comment on the presence of the Evil One: how does he set himself against Jesus? (no. 6).

II

The Church, Echo and Interpreter of God's Word

1. The Church's vital reference to the Word

7. In a passage of unusual depth and concision, Vatican II's *Constitution on Divine Revelation* stresses how vital is the Church's reference to the Word of God:

> The task of authentically interpreting the Word of God, whether written or handed on, has been entrusted exclusively to the living teaching office of the Church, whose authority is exercised in the name of Jesus Christ. This teaching office is not above the Word of God, but serves it, teaching only what has been handed on,
> listening to it devoutly,
> guarding it scrupulously,
> explaining it faithfully by divine commission
> and with the help of the Holy Spirit.
> It draws from this one deposit of faith everything which it presents for belief as divinely revealed. (no. 10)

The word of God comes to us in a unique fashion through the inspired Scriptures; but, at another level, it reaches us through the authentic teaching of the living Magisterium, which constantly draws inspiration from the Word as from an ever gushing spring.

And this teaching is incarnated and illustrated in the message of life which the saints offer us: their living example can be likened to a pictorial catechism or to the stained glass windows on which our ancestors used to read the Bible.

St John says of Jesus that 'his life was the light of men.' We must be able to catch his radiant light on the faces of those who faithfully reflect it. They speak to us through their writings and their lives. These words of life may be fragmentary, but they are echoes of the one Word, which we have to pick up on the various wave-lengths that transmit it to us.

2. Reading the Bible with the Church

8. Our topic is 'deliverance.' And in the sphere of deliverance, one feels how greatly the faithful need the help of the Church's living Magisterium to guide them in their reading and interpretation of God's Word, and also to avoid arbitrary and erratic interpretations. When we read Scripture, it is not easy to distinguish the purely cultural and historical elements from God's Message to mankind. How can one read *the* Word of God in the *many and varied* words of the biblical writers? This is indeed a complex question.

One cannot simply adduce a biblical text without first seriously examining its literary genre. This was already emphasized by Pius XII in his Encyclical *Divino Afflante Spiritu* (1943):

Let the interpreter use every care, and take advantage of every indication provided by the most recent research, in an endeavour to discern the distinctive genius of the sacred writer, his condition in life, the age in which he lived, the written or oral sources he may have used, and the literary forms he employed. He will thus be able better to discover who the sacred writer was and what he meant by what he wrote . . .

But frequently the literal sense is not so obvious in the words and writings of ancient oriental authors as it is with the writers of today. For what they intended to signify by their words is not determined only by the laws of grammar or philology, nor merely by their context. (no. 38)

It is impossible to overemphasize the necessity of an 'ecclesial' reading of the Bible, that is to say, the necessity of reading it in the light of the interpretation given by the Church's living Magisterium.

I know of no better exposition of this subject than the one given by Father George H. Tavard who, as a specialist in ecumenism, is very much alive to the problem. As he very justly points out:

Scripture cannot be the Word of God once it has been severed from the Church which is the Bride and the Body of Christ. And the Church could not be the Bride and the Body, had she not received the gift of understanding the Word. These two phases of God's visitation of man are aspects of one mystery. They are ultimately one, though one in two. The Church implies the Scripture as the Scripture implies the Church.[1]

3. Expressions of the ecclesial faith

9. The Church, as the interpreter of God's Word, expresses her faith in a variety of ways:

—Through her liturgical and sacramental life, which implies an understanding of God's Word. The well-known adage *lex orandi, lex credendi* makes this clear: the Church reveals her faith in her prayer.

—Through her ordinary living Magisterium, that is, through the common teaching of the college of Bishops in union with the Pope.

—Through a declaration of her extraordinary Magisterium—a declaration made in Council, for example to define the Church's position when there is a possible danger of heresy or deviation.

—Or again, through an *ex cathedra* pronouncement by the

Pope, who in this instance expresses and authenticates the faith of the Church.

The inspired Word comes to us, sustained and carried by the living Tradition of the doctors and saints, illuminated and authenticated by the Magisterium. This is the vital context in which the Christian life and the whole faith of the Church are steeped.

4. *The sacred texts complete each other*

10. Let us remember not to take the sacred texts in isolation, for they complete each other. There is a type of literature that cites texts indiscriminately to support the author's theory, but leaves out other, equally important passages which complete and give balance to the point under discussion. Jesus promises us his inexpressible peace, yet declares that he has come to bring not peace but the sword. He underlines the duty of honouring one's father, yet declares, in another passage that, in order to follow him, one must hate one's father and let the dead bury the dead. These are paradoxical, contrasting, but at the same time, complementary passages of the Gospel. A diamond has countless facets which sparkle in the sun, at times alternately, and at other times in one great blaze of light. 'I love contradictory things that exist simultaneously,' says a character of Claudel. All unilateralism is dangerous.

5. *The Old and the New Testaments*

11. We must bear in mind that Scripture, too, can be read from various standpoints or 'angles of light.' The Old Testament, while being an anticipation and prophecy of the New Testament, must be read in the light of the New Testament. The Gospel itself must be read, from the outset, in the light of Easter, which shines between the lines of each page.

In the tenebrous realm that concerns us here, these keys to the reading of Scripture are of special importance. If we disregard them, we may forget that the Gospel is the Good News.

So it is by following numerous convergent paths that we must reflect on the authentic teaching of the Church concerning the presence of the Evil One and the Powers of Darkness in the world.

As a further guide to the reading of the sacred texts, it is also important to be aware of the different periods in which they were written.

As I pointed out earlier, the viewpoint of ancient Israel was not the viewpoint of Judaism in Jesus' lifetime: let us remember this when we interpret the texts. And, even more importantly, the economy of the redemption was no longer the same after the Lord's paschal victory. By his Death and Resurrection, we have entered a new world: we share in the Power of the Spirit who acts in us through the grace of baptism. And only the Spirit can penetrate us in depth, in order to christianize us and to enable us to say with St Paul: 'I live—not I, but Christ in me' (Gal. 2:20). The same Paul recognizes that he is a sinner. The cause, he declares, is 'sin living in me' (Rom. 7:17). But never does he say that the Devil lives in him. For St Paul, sin is essentially man's refusal to let the Spirit of God act in him. And he makes this very clear in 1 Thess. 4:8: 'Whoever disregards this teaching, disregards not man but God, who gives you his Holy Spirit.'

What is foremost in the Church's mind is not the Devil, but deliverance from sin. And the Church has always been careful to stress this point.

6. *The Church as the interpreter of St Mark's text:* *'You will cast out demons'*

12. Again, it is the Church who must guide us in the reading of precise and specific texts concerning Jesus' promise to his future disciples that they would conquer the Powers of Evil. Let us pause to consider the ending of Mark's Gospel which, though added to the primitive text, is nonetheless included by the

Church in the canonically accepted body of inspired scripture and recognized as authentic apostolic witness. How should we read and interpret these words of the Master, which have parallels in other New Testament writings?

> These are the signs that will accompany believers: in my name they will cast out demons; they will speak in tongues; they will pick up snakes in their hands, and be unharmed should they drink deadly poison; they will lay their hands on the sick, who will recover. (Mark 16:17-18)

In the final reckoning, who else but the Church's living Magisterium can say what must be taken literally in this passage and what should be interpreted as hyperbolic images, urging the future disciples to put their trust in the Lord?

My purpose here is not to give a detailed interpretation of this text, but to consider a few points which occur to me, and which I offer as examples.

'You will cast out demons,' promises the Lord. Yes, undoubtedly, but there are numerous ways of triumphing over the Evil One.

—Jesus himself did not adopt a uniform, fixed method. He did not say that the demons should be adjured, as he himself sometimes adjured them (not always). He did not say that they should be commanded to reveal their names, or that the exorcist should try to discover their 'speciality,' not to mention the full details of their identity.

—During his public ministry, Jesus reacted in numerous ways when he came to grips with the Spirit of Evil. He manifested a sovereign freedom in his choice of means: at times he would pointedly ignore the demon and address the sick person; at other times, he would challenge the demon, denounce him as an impostor and order him to depart immediately.

—Jesus did not say that this fight against evil should be a single combat. He did not give his disciples the infallible formula for the discernment of spirits, or the unfailing method to be followed. But he created the apostolic ministry to guide them on their path, while awaiting his glorious return.

—Jesus did not say that direct grappling with the demon—the direct attack through a command or adjuration—was an integral part of the Christian life and that it was therefore advisable to teach all Christians 'deliverance' (as understood here). He did not say that 'deliverance' should be envisaged as a daily act of piety. Nor did he recommend that Christians be encouraged to 'pick up snakes in their hands' and to 'drink deadly poison.'

It is equally useful to note that no demon of lust was expelled from the adulterous woman (John 8), or from the woman of ill-repute mentioned by Luke (ch. 7), or from the incestuous people of Corinth (1 Cor. 5). No demon of avarice was expelled from Zacchaeus, no demon of incredulity from Peter after his triple betrayal. No demon of rivalry was expelled from the Corinthians whom Paul had to call to order.

The Lord did not say that the Devil is at the root of *all* human sin, and that all the sins of men are committed at his instigation. He told his disciples a parable which points to a very different teaching. The Parable of the Sower does mention situations where the Devil comes and removes the good seeds, but also others where the seeds die because they have fallen into shallow soil—a symbol of the superficiality and fickleness of men; or again, because they have been choked by thorns—a symbol of the cares of this world which turn men away from God (Matt. 13:19ff.; Mark 4:15; Luke 8:12ff.).

The Devil is fought positively and preventively by everything that nourishes and strengthens the Christian life, and therefore, above all, by recourse to the Sacraments.

Among these, the Eucharist—the centre of convergence of all the Sacraments—is for us Christians the supreme source of healing and liberation.

Just as the sun dispels the darkness of night through the full force of its blazing light, Christ Jesus unfolds in the eucharistic mystery all his power of life and victory over Evil.

In short, to understand a text, we have to set it in its full, vital context; and the final discernment, the interpretation that is faithful to both the Spirit and the letter of the text, falls to the Church's living Magisterium.

Note

1. G.H. Tavard, *Holy Writ or Holy Church* (London: Burns and Oates, 1959), p. 246.

Prayer

Let us ask with the Church's prayer for the grace not to stray as lone wanderers from her interpretation of the Word of God:

LORD, WATCH OVER YOUR CHURCH, AND GUIDE IT WITH YOUR UNFAILING LOVE. PROTECT US FROM WHAT COULD HARM US AND LEAD US TO WHAT WILL SAVE US. HELP US ALWAYS, FOR WITHOUT YOU WE ARE BOUND TO FAIL.

Prayer for Monday of the Second Week in Lent

+   +   +

Questions for reflection and discussion

1. People often say: 'Yes, I adhere to Jesus, but not to the Church.' Why is the union between Jesus and his Church indissoluble? (no. 7).

2. Why and how do we read Scripture 'with the Church' and not according to purely arbitrary personal interpretations which fail to realize that the texts complete one another? (nos. 8, 10 and 11).

3. Where do we find the diverse expressions of the Church's faith? (no. 9).

4. In the present chapter analyse the commentary on Jesus' words: 'You will cast out demons.' What does fighting the Devil 'positively and preventively' mean? (no. 12).

III

The Church and the 'Liberating' Sacramental Life

A. General Considerations

1. Jesus Christ's continuous presence

13. If Christ continues to act in a mysterious fashion by virtue of his ever-living and present Word, he also comes to us and acts powerfully in us through the sacraments.

Each sacrament is a Word of Christ, brought to its supreme degree of efficacy in an action of the Church. This presence of Jesus Christ is the very heart of the 'mystery of the Church.' It is at this precise point of our faith that the roads divide: some Christians look at the Church with the eyes of a sociologist or an historian and class her among the purely human 'institutions,' while others look at her with the eyes of faith, and reach beyond her inevitably deficient human aspects in order to see Christ, working through the ministry of men.

The first and fundamental chapter of *Lumen Gentium*, Vatican II's *Constitution on the Church*, sets forth the Church as a 'mystery of God.' This initial chapter, which conditions the whole Constitution, has remained practically unknown to Christians because we have failed to teach its message adequately. If we wish to 'christianize' Christians, we must help them to rediscover Jesus' operative presence in the Church and the sacramental 'virtue' whose source lies in him.

Since Jesus is the Sacrament of the Father—he who brings us into the Father's intimacy and reveals him—Vatican Council II, speaking of the Church analogically and at her own level, has called her 'the universal sacrament of salvation' (L.G., n. 48, s2), or again 'the sacrament in Jesus Christ of intimate union with God, and of the unity of all mankind' (L.G., n. 1).

These words express the basic truth of her being, her identity which conditions her action. Jesus Christ founded the Church so that she may perpetuate not his historical presence, but his spiritual presence as the Risen Lord. It was not merely the thirty-three or so years of his earthly life that he filled with his presence: his action transcends the centuries and will remain with us until the end of time. It is through and in the Word and the sacraments that Jesus continues to act among us.

As the Church Fathers repeatedly stressed, it is not the priest who baptizes, consecrates, absolves and heals, but Christ himself, acting in and through the priestly ministry.

Beneath the Church's sacramental action lies the action of Christ, working through his Spirit. To neglect or minimize our contact with the Church's sacramental ministry is to deprive ourselves of our first and normal sources of life.

2. *A liberating presence*

14. Our source of life is, by the same token, a source of healing extended to everything that endangers the divine life in us; it is a source of liberation from the onslaughts of sin and evil, and the prime source of deliverance from the Evil One. Through her sacramental action the Church is fundamentally a mystery of salvation.

Each sacrament is given to us so that Jesus may complete his work in us, extend to us the fruits of his redeeming passion, and create that new humanity which he wishes to offer his Father and has already won at the price of his blood.

We should analyse the Church's sacraments one by one, in order to grasp the power of life contained in each sacrament, and also the immanent grace of healing and immunization against the work of the Evil One.

Such an exploration brings us to the heart of the Church, as the sacrament of salvation and liberation. It is there that we encounter God's saving grace, not exclusively, but primarily and at its greatest depth of action and influence. It is impossible to exaggerate the significance of the sacraments as a means of responding to and welcoming God's vivifying and purifying action.

3. Not automatism

15. But if the sacraments are operative through their intrinsic virtue—*ex opere operato*—they must never be envisaged as automatic: it is a serious mistake to take the sacraments for granted, that is to say, to neglect or minimize the preparation or reception, and not to respect the Christian demands they make on our lives.

We too easily become accustomed to the instruments of grace at our disposal. Formalism and complacency are ever-present temptations: we must constantly review the way in which we live the sacramental life in our everyday conduct and relationships.

We have to examine our conscience regularly. When faced with the question: why do the young so frequently turn away from the Church?, one may cite a series of causes extrinsic to the Church community, such as the moral decadence and dechristianization of the world around us. And all this is perfectly true. But there are also intrinsic causes which stem from our own conduct, and more particularly from the way we incorporate the sacramental life into our everyday existence. We are still far too dominated by sheer habit, routine. Too much dead wood prevents trees from blossoming.

The liturgical renewal has not yet achieved its full goal, for in reality it reaches far beyond the adoption of the vernacular and a few liturgical innovations. The sense of worship, of thanks-

giving, of reconciliation through prayer and brotherly fellow-
ship still has to be restored in depth.

Why are so many young people looking for spiritual nourishment elsewhere—in sects, in esoteric doctrines? Are they not
implicitly appealing for a sacramental life that ties up with life
itself, as they know it?

At this level, too, I see the Charismatic Renewal as a grace
that can revitalize Christians, and therefore as a golden
opportunity.

Returning to our topic, deliverance, let us bring out and
throw into bold relief that liberating grace which lies at the heart
of each sacrament and is offered to us. Let us grasp the extent to
which the fight against Evil and its influence is an integral part
of the life of the sacramental Church.

The following brief analysis of the role of Baptism, the
Eucharist and Penance will illustrate my point.

B. Particular Considerations

1. Baptism

16. Baptism radically associates us with the Saviour's Death
and Resurrection; it is in the highest sense a sacrament of
liberation and deliverance. It involves a very explicit renunciation of Satan and his works, which, incidentally, does not mean
that demonic possession is thought to be present, but implies
that the newly born Christian already makes Christ's victory
over Evil his own victory.

In the rite of infant Baptism, the Church expresses herself as
follows:

Almighty God, you sent your only Son to rescue us from the
slavery of sin, and to give us the freedom only your sons and
daughters enjoy. We now pray for these children who will
have to face the world with its temptations, and fight the
devil in all his cunning. Your Son died and rose again to save
us. By his victory over sin and death, bring these children out

of the powers of darkness. Strengthen them with the grace of Christ, and watch over them at every step in life's journey.

In the rite of Baptism received in stages by adults, the proposed prayer of exorcism is worded thus: 'By the Spirit of truth, free all who struggle under the yoke of the father of lies.'

Turning now to the liturgy of Holy Saturday, let us look briefly at the Renewal of Baptismal Vows.

The celebrant asks the assembly the question involving the personal commitment of each member: 'Do you reject Satan? And all his works? And all his empty promises?' Their answer to such a challenging question is obviously of the highest consequence. But it can assume its full meaning only if Satan is perceived as a reality, and the Christian life as a spiritual battle against the Powers of Evil.

In unison the faithful reply 'I do.' But does our current teaching sufficiently bring home to them the full implications of their answer? Has our preaching told them that the paschal mystery is itself victory over Satan, sin and death? I fear not, and I too am guilty of this omission. Our current catechesis hardly prepares the Christian people to grasp the import and implications of this dialogue.

The next Synod of Bishops in Rome, which will be devoted to the theme of Reconciliation and Penance, could also, I feel, very usefully study the question of how this Holy Saturday dialogue can be better prepared, better understood, and lived at a deeper level. The liturgy has everything to gain by being more concrete and realistic.

2. The Eucharist

17. The Eucharist, 'the source and the apex of the Christian life' (Vatican II), the source from which everything flows and the centre towards which all the sacraments converge, is preeminently a participation in the paschal mystery of the Lord's Death and Resurrection. It is steeped in his redeeming sacrifice and, by that very fact, it is the source of the new life and of the healing of body and soul, the sacrament of liberation.

Before taking communion, the priest addresses this prayer to the Lord: 'May your body and blood deliver me from my sins and from every evil.' The evil to which he refers encompasses all the living forces of Evil. The Eucharist is the antidote to those evil forces: it is 'the remedy of immortality,' the pledge of our future resurrection, and the communion *par excellence* with our Liberator.

In the Eucharist we celebrate the power of Jesus who conquers all the forces of Evil. In him our own passover—our passing from death to life—is already accomplished.

The Eucharist is a paschal celebration in which the emphasis is laid on the victory won by the Saviour's death; a celebration in which we worship the Father 'through Him, with Him, in Him,' and in the joy of knowing that we are redeemed and liberated, even though we have not yet reached the final stage of the journey. A keen awareness of the paschal mystery is incompatible with a pessimistic vision of creation and the world, and also with the affirmation of man's intrinsic perversion which, as we know, is strongly underlined in the tradition born of the Protestant Reformation. In Part Three I shall return to the subject of the Eucharist as victory over the Powers of Evil.

3. Penance

18. The sacrament of Penance or Reconciliation is more than a sacrament of forgiveness: not only does it efface sin, but it gives grace and a power of resistance in the struggles yet to come. It frees us from sin which gives the forces of Evil their ascendancy over us.

The sacrament of Penance, which the Lord entrusted to his apostles, is a sacrament of healing, willed by the Lord so that we may experience his mercy and love: it is a privileged instrument for conquering sin and its slavery. Received in the right disposition, it achieves the sinner's conversion and inner liberation. It is eminently a ministry of deliverance.

For the faithful all this is basic doctrine. But our common

task is to actualize all the potentials of the sacrament of Penance, and the experience of Christians could help considerably to give it more realism and a greater repercussion on life itself. A dialogue between the 'teaching' and the 'taught' Church on this point would be enriching and beneficial. For we must constantly endeavour to integrate the sacraments into our lives and not give them a marginal place. As we know, some Free Churches, being unacquainted with the sacramental resources of deliverance, have given its practice an autonomy and scope of doubtful wisdom. But, for our part, we must enrich and vivify our sacramental pastoral practice, particularly in regard to the sacrament of Reconciliation. Here, too, the next Synod of Bishops could be an instrument of grace.

4. *The Anointing of the Sick*

Equally relevant to our theme is the sacrament of anointing the sick, the sacrament of spiritual, if not physical, healing. As such, it has its own power in the sphere of deliverance. I hope to return to this subject in a subsequent Malines Document which, God willing, will be devoted to the charism and ministry of healing.

C. The Sacramentals

19. In the line of the sacraments, the Church recognizes the use of sacramentals, provided that one is careful to avoid any exaggerated use or interpretation of them.

In its *Constitution on the Sacred Liturgy*, Vatican II has reminded the faithful of the legitimacy of the sacramentals, while urging that, when necessary, they be adjusted to the requirements of our time.

This is the relevant passage:

Holy Mother Church has, moreover, instituted sacramentals. These are sacred signs which bear a resemblance to the sacraments: they signify effects, particularly of a spiritual kind, which are obtained through the Church's intercession. By them men are disposed to receive the chief effect of the sacraments, and various occasions in life are rendered holy. (C.S.L., n. 60)

The Council goes on to underline, in this connection, the pastoral value of the liturgy and its relation to the paschal mystery:

> Thus, for well-disposed members of the faithful, the liturgy of the sacraments and sacramentals sanctifies almost every event in their lives; they are given access to the stream of divine grace which flows from the paschal mystery of the passion, death and resurrection of Christ, the fountain from which all sacraments and sacramentals draw their power. There is hardly any proper use of material things which cannot thus be directed towards the sanctification of men and the praise of God. (C.S.L., n. 61)

The Church therefore recognizes the legitimate place of the sacramentals in her life—a subordinate and relative place, no doubt, but nonetheless real.

In the logic of the Incarnation of God's Son, who took on our human nature, it is only normal that this sanctifying and liberating action should be prolonged not only through the sacraments, but also through humble human symbols, sanctified by the Church's petitionary prayer.

The use of the sign of the Cross, holy water, holy oil, blessed palms, etc., has nothing to do with magic rites. Using them in a spirit of faith, as a symbolic prayer of deliverance, is all part of the spiritual patrimony recognized by the Church.

The sign of the Cross, in particular, is at once the expression of our trinitarian faith and an armour against the Powers of Evil, in the line of St Paul's recommendation:

> Put on the whole armour of God, that you may be able to stand against the wiles of the devil. . . . Always carry the

shield of faith, with which you can quench all the flaming darts of the evil one. (Eph. 6:11, 16)

+   +   +

Prayer

Let us ask the Lord, in a prayer of the Church, to lead us to the source of all liberation:

MAY THE HOLY COMMUNION WE HAVE RECEIVED, LORD, SAVE US FROM OUR SINS AND KEEP US FOR EVER IN THE LIGHT OF YOUR TRUTH.

Postcommunion for the Nineteenth Sunday of the Ordinary Time of the Year

+   +   +

Questions for reflection and discussion

1. Jesus' historical presence is continued today in his sacramental presence. Try to express how Christ works in the heart of the sacraments (no. 13).

2. How can we avoid using the sacraments automatically, or without preparing ourselves fittingly? (no. 10).

3. How can the Renewal contribute to the valorization of the sacramental life? (nos. 16-19).

4. Show the eminent role and place of the Eucharist as 'deliverance from evil' (no. 17).

IV

The Church Faced with 'the Mystery of Iniquity'

1. Sin, the first enemy

20. Demonological literature usually focuses on real or supposed cases of diabolic possession. The mass media, for their part, have strongly accentuated this tendency.

We must realize that very frequently the scenes portrayed are distorted visions of reality, and we must avoid the danger of attributing undue importance to what is in fact rare and exceptional.

What makes us 'slaves' of the Powers of Evil is not normally 'demonic possession.' All theologians agree that the Devil cannot penetrate into the intimate depths of the soul unless the subject voluntarily surrenders them to him.

It is sin and its hold on us which make us slaves and allow perverse influences to become more and more harmful, as a wind fans the flames of an imprudently lit fire. The Devil's most deadly weapon *is not the grip he may have on man, but sin itself.*

His influence is present wherever sin reigns and, alas, sin has invaded our humanity, now unbalanced and straying in unwonted moral permissiveness.

So deliverance is basically and primarily *deliverance from the*

31

sin in us, which makes us slaves and diminishes our freedom. The slavery of sin affects every human faculty: reason, will, action, emotion. This type of enslavement has a wide field of influence and takes countless forms.

It is on this basic fact, and not on phenomena which may be purely psychopathological, that we must focus our attention when we speak of deliverance. As Jean-Claude Sagne, O.P., writes:

> It is in the void caused by our lack of trust in God or by our egoistic attachments, or again by our proud self-sufficiency, that the devil intervenes to transform our weakness into a spiritual burden, to make our attachments spiritual 'bonds' and, last but not least, to turn our arrogant impulses into an obstacle that stands firm against the invasion of the Holy Spirit. Much could be said about the enticements of the devil and the bad angels who support him. Satan hardens what he lays hands on and disorganizes it even more. He accentuates already engrained tendencies. He exploits our weaknesses. . . . [1]

2. Concupiscence

21. Let us remember, too, that within us there is a force which cannot be equated with sin but is an element of disturbance, not necessarily of the demonic kind. I am speaking of concupiscence.

Theology usually takes this term to mean the effects left by sin in man already justified by grace, that is to say, the aftereffects which resist his will and take the form of various drives. There we have a time-honoured theological definition: it describes a situation which precedes the exercise of freedom and partly conditions justified man's moral behaviour. St Paul did not hesitate to write: 'I fail to carry out the things I want to do, and I find myself doing the very things I hate' (Rom. 7:15).

Concupiscence, which underlies human activity, must not be identified with a special and direct hold on man by the Devil.

3. 'Structural' sin

22. What holds true of individuals is equally true of our society's antihuman structures—whether economic, social or political—which violate human rights and are incompatible with man's dignity. Sin reigns at this level, too, even if it is difficult to make a clear distinction between individual and collective responsibility.

We too readily imagine that the Devil's action is always of a sensational nature. In fact, his conspicuous interventions are exceptional. And precisely because his action is invisible and subtle, it is all the more perverse.

4. Man is primarily responsible

23. Radical pessimism about the world, the human body and man's fundamental freedom has no place in the Catholic faith. Though wounded by sin, man is primarily responsible for his actions and he is not the passive toy of demonic influences which try to manipulate him.

The Devil exercises his influence in a variety of ways: he is the tempter, the seducer, the inspirer of sinful decisions. He deceives and, 'disguised as an angel of light' (2 Cor. 11:14), presents evil as virtue, falsehood as truth.

But he does not have a despotic ascendancy over man: he needs the consent of those he tries to subjugate and, in the final analysis, man is always responsible for his sin.

The emphasis laid on demonic influences must not serve as an excuse or a cover-up for human weakness and diminish or destroy our awareness of our responsibility. It is all too convenient to adduce causes extrinsic to ourselves in order to tone down or attenuate our personal freedom of decision. The Church has always been opposed to everything that 'destabilizes' man and makes him the plaything of alien forces. She teaches that God has placed our fate in our own hands by creating us free and responsible, and that if man's responsibility can be attenuated by circumstances, it nonetheless remains basically intact.

5. *Faith, the supreme safeguard*

24. As for the Devil, he welcomes everything that prevents man from adhering to God. His usual strategy can be summed up as follows: the Devil makes every effort to conceal God from man.

To prevent us from reaching God and living in his light, the Devil's favourite method is to attack the root of all Christian living: our God-centered faith. For our faith puts us in direct contact with God, and the Devil cannot enter this realm which is reserved for God alone. The more man lives by faith, the more he is impervious to the Devil's attacks: faith is a fortress which protects man from his onslaughts, and that is why he endeavours to bring the believer out of the fortress by dazzling him with a host of illusory enticements, as would a conjurer, and by tempting him to rely on something more sensational than pure faith.

This is undoubtedly the danger of the 'visions,' 'revelations' and 'prophecies' which abound in our world and which the Charismatic Renewal must approach cautiously. One may safely presume that, in most cases, they are fruits of the imagination, and it is the Church's task to discern them in order to avoid the danger of illuminism. These counterfeits of the supernatural constitute a sphere that is particularly accessible to the maneuvers of the Spirit of Evil.

In the final reckoning, one may well wonder whether the sensational way of presenting Satan's work in this world might not also be a trick of the Devil, who thus gives those who deny his existence a further argument in support of their negations.

6. The 'mystery of iniquity'

(a) On the invisible plane

25. The world of darkness is by definition a tenebrous realm which cannot be directly grasped by the human mind.

Doubtless the mystery of God is also unseeable, but for quite another reason: here below our eyes are too weak to bear its dazzling light. Who can fathom the mystery of God's creative, redeeming and sanctifying love?

But the 'mystery of iniquity,' of which St Paul speaks, is of a very different nature: it is impenetrable precisely because it is shrouded in darkness. No man can penetrate it, even with the aid of the strongest torch.

This sphere, more than any other, must be approached with discretion and sobriety if we wish to speak of it adequately. Let us take care not to introduce into the realm of darkness our always analogical and deficient human concepts, our logic and classifications. On this subject there is a certain literature so full of pseudo-certitudes that at every page one wants to cry out: 'Be careful!'

Francis MacNutt, one of the authors who, in my view, have excessively popularized in the Catholic Charismatic Renewal the subject of demonic influences, rightly points out—while often forgetting it in practice—that every demonic manifestation is ambiguous, and that no symptom or set of symptoms are in themselves a convincing proof of specifically demonic activity. It is undeniable that here we are in the realm of darkness, of pure irrationality—a realm which, by definition, no human mind can grasp.[2]

(b) On the visible plane

26. Although the mystery of iniquity is usually enacted in darkness, there are times when it becomes glaringly obvious.

Traces of the Church's belief in diabolic manifestations are found in the liturgy, the rites, patristics, and also in the lives of historical figures: the Desert Fathers, the anchorites, and numerous monks and saints. History has left us innumerable accounts which, though coloured by the spirit or naivety of their time, must hold our attention by the very fact of their continuity.

The permanence of the phenomenon of diabolic manifestations, whether they be true or false, raises many questions.

For they are found throughout history and in a wide variety of forms. In particular, they crop up in the lives of the most diverse saints, such as Benedict, Francis, John of God, Vincent Ferrier, Peter of Alcantara, and also in the lives of such female saints as Margaret of Cordova, Angela of Foligno, Rita of Cascia, Rose of Lima, and many others.

Nearer to our time, in the nineteenth century, the life of the Cure d'Ars was full of temptations which he suffered as cruel and severe 'plagues.' The hagiographers speak of unusual and alarming noises which prevented him from sleeping, of vexations and threats, of vulgar abuse, of blows and all manner of affronts. All this is attributed to the Spirit of Darkness.

In the twentieth century I would merely cite, as an example, the life of Padre Pio, the famous stigmatist who died in 1968 and whose cause is under examination. It contains numerous references to demonic attacks: the devil appeared to Padre Pio in dreadful forms, torturing him, throwing him out of his bed, and making similar onslaughts on many occasions.

What may we conclude from the permanence of these phenomena? In essence, I reply: here we are dealing with the realm of darkness and we have to advance with extreme prudence. One cannot avoid the question: how does one distinguish the cases of psychiatric disturbance from those that clearly denote diabolic influences? To judge the matter, we have few firm and decisive criteria. All we can say is that it is not reasonable to accept all these phenomena outright as diabolic manifestations—this being the temptation of supernaturalism; but neither is it reasonable to dismiss them out of hand as hysterical or hallucinatory disturbances—this being the temptation of rationalism.

Notes

1. J.C. Sagne, O.P., 'La Prière de dèlivrance et de guèrison,' in *Tychique*, no. 23, 1980.
2. Cf. B. Lonergan, *Insight: 666 on Basic Evil*, London-New York, 1957.

✝   ✝   ✝

Prayer

Let us ask the Lord to give us his liberating healing:

LORD, IN YOUR MERCY GRANT THAT YOUR HEALING GRACE MAY FREE US FROM OUR EVIL INCLINATIONS AND LEAD US TOWARDS TRUE HOLINESS.

Postcommunion for the Tenth Sunday of the Ordinary Time of the Year

✝   ✝   ✝

Questions for reflection and discussion

1. The devil's most fearful weapon is not 'demonic possession' but sin as such. Explain this statement (no. 20).

2. Why must we strongly underline that God has placed our fate in our hands by creating us free and responsible? What practical consequences flow from our responsible freedom where demonic influences are concerned? (no. 23).

3. Walking in faith protects us from the temptation to overemphasize extraordinary or sensational phenomena. Explain this statement (no. 24).

4. By definition the 'mystery of iniquity' eludes our classifications and we must speak of it very soberly and discreetly. See no. 25 and compare with the points made in chapter 8.

V

The Church Confronted
with Sin

1. Sin in the heart of the world

27. The very concept of sin, as opposition to the divine will and a breach of friendship with God, the Creator and Father of men, is vanishing in today's world.

Predictably, an American author has written an important book significantly entitled *Whatever Became of Sin.* [1]

It is, in any case, not surprising that we are losing the sense of sin in proportion as our sense of God and the Gospel is declining. Sin is an abyss which cannot be fathomed by human reason alone. To measure it adequately, we need to understand both the transcendence and the immanence of God: what he is in himself, and what he is in us.

It is said that Ozanam, whose son was reproaching him for having called himself a great sinner, replied: 'My son, you don't understand what God's holiness is!' We have to be very close to God to measure the distance that separates us from him.

We have a poor appreciation of God's transcendence, and also of his immanence. It is in his immanence that he identifies himself with us when we serve him in our neighbour and he tells me: 'You should have done this to *me.*'

Who then is God, sings the poet, whom no one can love
   unless he loves man?

39

Who then is God whom we can wound so deeply
by wounding man?

We can also approach the abyss of sin from another angle: by
contemplating Christ dying on Calvary, 'the Lamb who takes
away the sin of the world, the Saviour who gives up his life for
the forgiveness of sins.'

Sin has to be viewed in the light of God, otherwise it becomes
meaningless. And all the more so as the Freudian analyses have
removed man's responsibility for sin by relegating evil to the
unconscious or to the domain of psychopathology.

Modern man no longer understands the religious dimension
of sin. Good and evil no longer depend on anything but his own
interpretations: he is his own law and 'the measure of all things.'
The mere fact of not doing harm to others frees him from any
higher law. But this is to forget that the person who degrades
himself, even in secret, debases humanity. There is deep
meaning in this saying of Elisabeth Lesueur: 'The person who
lifts himself up to God also lifts up the whole world.' The
contrary is equally true: we are bound to one another, in good as
in evil, by a mysterious interdependence. Every action affects
the whole world. Epidemics and nuclear fallouts are not the
only things that cross the frontiers of nations.

28. Sociological inquiries and surveys are incapable of
revealing the true mainspring of the world's disorders which,
basically, is quite simply the sin of men.

For it is sin which, in the last analysis, is the source of all the
social evils and wrongs that are ceaselessly regenerated under
every latitude and regime. Sin is not only disorder in relation to
God; it is nihilistic and antisocial by its very nature. As I said
earlier, the man who commits sin—even in secret—is under-
mining society, because he is damaging and dehumanizing
mankind.

The Pastoral Constitution *Gaudium et Spes* strongly empha-
sizes this link between personal sin and social damage:

Certainly, the disturbances which so frequently occur in the social order result in part from the natural tensions of economic, political and social forms. But at a deeper level they flow from man's pride and selfishness, which contaminate even the social sphere. (n. 25)

Every sin, moreover, strengthens Satan's hold on this world. It is through sin that the 'Prince of lies' discovers the weak spots which allow him to exacerbate the conflicts of men, to set them against each other, and to fuel our inevitably fratricidal wars. For as the Bible tells us, 'he was a murderer from the beginning.' Sin is at the heart of the drama of men, whether they know it or not, whether they acknowledge it or deny it.

2. *The current moral degradation*

29. Before describing the moral degradation that we are witnessing today, it is only fair to commend the real advances of the human conscience in a wide range of charitable and social undertakings. In particular, we note a refinement of man's awareness and sense of solidarity, and a worldwide alertness in the vast field of human rights, even if in practice those same rights are cynically violated every day in certain countries.

But, under the cover of human rights, we are also witnessing in vital areas, alas, an unprecedented moral breakdown which is shaking the foundations of all social life.

No longer interpreting good and evil in reference to God and the Gospel, man has made himself the supreme criterion of good and evil.

Once the floodgates are opened, the consequences of this wholly relative view are particularly obvious in the most vulnerable spheres of man's existence: respect for human life and respect for authentic love. Let us pause for a moment to consider these two very sensitive areas.

(a) Respect for nascent human life

The decision—supported by a large majority—that in many cases procured abortion will henceforth be legal and covered by Social Security has triggered off a series of dangers which lead to the worst consequences. Once nascent life is sacrificed to suit the convenience of individuals, there is no logical reason why our future societies should respect the right to life of the handicapped, of patients with incurable illnesses, of 'useless' aged people, and so on. A persuasive and persevering campaign launched by the mass media could, by manipulating public opinion, ultimately sweep away the entire moral heritage bequeathed to us by the Gospel—a heritage which is, in fact, the foundation of our civilization.

(b) Respect for love

30. The family, thus attacked at its root, is also threatened by the 'right to free love,' which has become another major claim of our society. This view of love explains the present sharp increase in divorce and already accounts, in some countries, for the breakdown of one marriage out of three. The dire consequences of this breakdown of the family are also seen in the alarming increase in juvenile delinquency—the fruit of these broken homes—and in drug addiction, violence, etc.

The wrong use of the word 'love' is responsible for the measureless confusion which prevails today in this area. In my book *Love and Control* (1960) I wrote:

For today's Christian, the word 'love' is a defeat whose losses must be recouped. The fact is that no other word has been so weakened and muddled by modern literature and the jargon used by television, radio, films and advertising. Newspapers and magazines are filled with it; every page has 'all the facts' about its 'amazing powers' and the crimes it inspires. Every day and all day, the radio broadcasts it, with or without music, on every wave-length. The cinema gives us love scenes lasting almost as long as entire films. Many plays revolve about it as their theme and the advertising world has undertaken to bring its 'new image' to the world.

'Love' is put forth as the one excuse which makes any sort of behaviour blameless, and which is its own justification. When a man is overwhelmed by desire for someone else's wife, he justifies his liberty by appealing to 'love.' People use it to cover up the most disgraceful conduct. But that is not real love; it is nothing more than blinding physical passion. 'Love' is used as an alibi, a cover-up for the most cynical selfishness, misconduct, adultery, impurity.

But this moral degradation is even more far-reaching. One is bound to agree with the following comment by Father Gerard Defois, Secretary of the French Episcopal Conference:

When love is reduced to a fleeting passion, sexuality to a cheap and momentary consumer product, the family to an ephemeral arrangement, man himself is stunted and pared down to the scale of a fear-ridden society. . . . Our disputes over contraception, abortion, divorce—in short, life itself— are just as important as our debates on armament and torture. Or more precisely, they are part of one and the same life-and-death struggle to give the family and our national or international concord a truly human quality.

3. *Waning of the sense of sin in the Christian conscience*

31. A particular drama is being enacted at this moment in the conscience of Christians themselves: the very notion of sin is dangerously waning.

Admittedly, our eucharistic liturgies still begin with the *Confiteor,* and the believer ritually strikes his breast. We still ask God in the *Our Father* to 'forgive us our sins and deliver us from evil'; and in the *Hail Mary* the 'Pray for us sinners' has not been suppressed.

But dare we say in all sincerity that we approach God 'with a contrite and humble heart,' though our lips confess it?

We must honestly ask ourselves: where do we stand in the matter of a specifically Christian morality? I say 'specifically Christian' advisedly, for I know that even this distinctive feature is queried in our ranks and that some maintain that there is no such thing.

We are not asked to examine the conscience of non-Christians. Let us begin by examining our own—that will suffice.

The air around us cannot be breathed with impunity. Immunity from it is all the more impossible as its miasmas reach us through the many channels of the mass media, those new regulators of the human conscience. To measure their influence, we need only look at the sphere of family life.

On what wave-length are we at this level? Where do we find our criteria for evaluating the significance of the family? Shall we disregard the teaching which the Church has recently given us in John Paul II's Encyclical *Familiaris Consortio*? Or shall we, on the contrary, welcome it and integrate it into our action as an essential and vital element of Christian behaviour? One is justified in questioning how it will be received.

In matters such as precocious sexual relations, information about contraception for all purposes, procured abortion, sexual deviations, lesbianism and homosexuality, juvenile cohabitation, trial marriage (in two or three stages), the very idea that all these forms of behaviour are not left to the whims of men, that there is a divine law, a Word of God, interpreted by the Magisterium, seems to have become quite alien to the conscience of many Christians, who are more concerned with modernization than with fidelity to doctrine.

While writing this, I happened to glance through a Christian review containing the following astonishing lines:

> Would it not be possible, on the religious plane in particular, to revise the pastoral teaching on marriage, bearing in mind (as people do today) the stages which the seriously considered building up of a love undergoes? Cohabitation with a firm

purpose, declaration before the Christian community that welcomes the couple. And lastly, the founding of a family when procreation has been decided upon, the latter postulating a deliberate desire for stability and duration. This would in no way prevent marriage, as a directly undertaken and binding commitment, for those who set their heart on it.

Without judging individual intentions, I must stress that this waning of the Christian sense of love and marriage is all the more serious as 'only love builds the world' and 'humanity's future depends on the family,' to quote John Paul II.

By persistently modelling our morality on the contagious customs of the moment—while awaiting tomorrow's practices, which may have even more dismal surprises in store for us—we are gradually losing our identity: this is the measure of our regression. It may well be that in today's 'Christian' world the Devil is very seldom exorcized, but there is no denying that we are exorcizing sin, and on a very wide scale.

4. A cry of warning

32. The most serious aspect of all this, I feel, is that Christians seem resigned to float aimlessly on this receding moral tide without protesting, without even reacting except by heaving a sigh and yielding to the inevitable. Defeatism is incompatible with our Christian mission in and for the world. Jesus told his disciples that though he was leaving them in the world, they could not be of the world. To compromise with evil, or to resign ourselves to it, is to deny our Christian identity.

Action and reaction are imperatives; today they are more essential than ever. We have to translate our prayer into action and to serve the Lord with fearless devotion. It is far better to speak of sin than of the devils, and to denounce the ravages of sin.

Our Alleluias will not be genuine unless, on leaving a prayer meeting, we seek together, with courage and imagination, how best to make the Gospel's demands resound in the heart of the world. This calls for a concrete strategy on the individual and collective ways and means of carrying out our specific task. There are numerous ways of protesting and of influencing those who hold the fate of a country in their hands. And we can learn something each day by observing the performance of those who are visibly destroying our moral heritage. The Lord said that 'the children of darkness are more astute than the children of light.' These words should stir our imagination and inspire courage in us. We need vigorous Christians, not only in those lands where they risk martyrdom daily, but also in our democratic countries, in our public life, where freedom still has its rights but, by the same token, makes demands on us.

Note

1. Karl Menninger, M.D., *Whatever Became of Sin?*, New York, Hawthorn Books, 1973.

Prayer

Faced with sin, the Church invites us to call incessantly on the Lord:

ALL-POWERFUL GOD, MAY THE WONDERFUL HUMAN BIRTH OF YOUR SON FREE US FROM OUR FORMER SLAVERY TO SIN AND BRING US TO NEW LIFE.

Prayer for the Sixth Day in the Octave of Christmas

+ + +

Questions for reflection and discussion

1. What is the direct or indirect relation between sin and the world's social and political disorders? (cf. nos. 22 and 28).

2. Which spheres of life are being particularly affected today by the moral degradation of man and society? (cf. nos. 29, 30, 31).

3. How can we best restore our fellow Christians' awareness of the reality of sin and reflect on the theme of the 1983 Synod of Bishops: 'Penance and Reconciliation?'

4. How can we react against the degradation of morals, personally and collectively, at all levels (press, radio, television) and alert those responsible for our public life? Concrete suggestions.

Part Two

Charismatic Renewal
and 'The Powers of Darkness'

VI

The Charismatic Renewal As 'Experience' of the Holy Spirit

1. The meaning of the term 'charismatic'

33. Before stating why the Charismatic Renewal has awakened a clearer awareness of the Spirit of Evil and sin in the world, I would like to explain briefly how and why it has contributed, positively, to a keener awareness of the Holy Spirit and his gifts. The positive and the negative aspects go together like the obverse and reverse of a coin. But first we must define our vocabulary.

The term 'charismatic' features in the above title, but elsewhere in this book I have used it sparingly so as not to overburden the text. Nevertheless, it needs to be clarified. In itself this word has no exclusive meaning: the whole Church is charismatic, and so is each Christian by virtue of his Baptism. But it has assumed an historical meaning and designates a particular movement which is often called 'the Renewal in the Spirit.' I prefer the latter title, for the word 'charismatic' does not cover all the aspects of this current spiritual renewal, which bears not only on the domain of the Holy Spirit's charisms, but on many other features of the Christian life.

Because every genuine renewal depends on the Holy Spirit, all the spiritual movements in the Church can rightly be called 'charismatic.' But history has reserved this adjective for a particular Renewal, which began in 1967 and stemmed from prayer groups in the United States.

I would add that it is not an 'organized' movement in the accepted sense of the word. It has no founder, no 'institutionalized' leaders, and it does not form a homogeneous whole. Consequently, the practice of deliverance varies according to countries and cultures. This diversity must be borne in mind, for it explains why some of the warnings given here are particularly applicable to local situations.

2. The basic experience of the Renewal

34. Let me begin by describing the basic experience which is the soul of the Renewal. Progressing beyond superficial analogies, we have to understand the Renewal as a grace that reactualizes baptism and confirmation, as a kind of personal Pentecost involving conversion, a re-acknowledgement of Jesus Christ, a new openness to the Holy Spirit. Inevitably, most definitions are incomplete, and it is up to the theologians to look for the best formulation. The danger of the term 'baptism in the Spirit' is that it may cause us to overlook the one Baptism which incorporates us into the life of Christ; in the same way, the term 'personal Pentecost' must never allow us to forget that Pentecost, the day on which the Church was founded, remains a unique event.

But whatever expressions we use, the fact is that an experience of conversion to a new life is clearly seen in the Church. It is sweeping through the five continents like a breath of profound rechristianization, like a wind fanning the smouldering embers and rekindling them into a blazing fire. 'I have come to cast fire upon the earth,' said Jesus, 'and would that it were already kindled!'

In response to the prayer of John XXIII and Paul VI, this religious awakening is continuing the mystery of Pentecost—not exclusively, but in a memorable way. What is new for those who have welcomed it is that the Holy Spirit, the permanent object of our faith, has become a living experience for them. This is the mainspring of the Renewal.

As Father Sullivan, S.J., Professor of Theology at the Gregorian University, writes:

> The Charismatics do not for a moment question that the Holy Spirit is given in the sacraments of Baptism and Confirmation and that he dwells in everyone who is living in the grace of Christ. At the same time, they believe that the Spirit, even though already present, can become present to the same person in a decisively new way; that is, by making his presence, previously a matter of faith, now a matter of experience:
> —by new manifestations of his working in that person's life;
> —by a striking increase of that person's power to bear Christian witness;
> —even by conferring charismatic gifts.
> It seems undeniable that such a new presence of the Holy Spirit in a Christian's life would be a precious gift of grace. . . . Their interpretation of their 'baptism in the Spirit' is that it is the initial experience of such a new presence and working of the Spirit in their lives.
> Looking, as they do, on the distinctive pentecostal experience as the beginning of a new presence of the Spirit, they insist that the emphasis should be put, not on the initial experience as such, but rather on the 'new life in the Spirit' that should follow upon it and must be nourished and sustained, if the original experience is going to bear its fruits.[1]

35. To this analysis—this testimony—I would like to add the following lines by a historian, Richard Quedebaux, who, in his book *The New Charismatics,* very accurately defines the implications of the charismatic experience:

> When Christ promised his disciples that he would bestow upon them the Holy Spirit after departing from them, he

anticipated three practical needs the Spirit would satisfy in their lives:

1. confirm faith,
2. bring joy in the midst of suffering and
3. assure, guide and teach those who would choose to follow Christ.

—Yet to many, if not most Christians, Christ's promise of his indwelling Spirit may be accepted intellectually, but it is not received experientially.

—Hence the promise is meaningless, and the question is raised again and again: How do I *know* that the Holy Spirit dwells within me?

—Charismatic Renewal offers an answer to the question. The baptism of the Holy Spirit, a powerful experience that convinces the recipient that God is real, that God is faithful to what he has promised and that the same 'signs and wonders,' described in the Book of Acts, can happen to-day, to *me*. [2]

Such is the Renewal's contribution to the keener awareness of the Holy Spirit acting in the Christian life.

This ever-present action of the Spirit is indeed what struck Pope John Paul I, to whom I had sent my book *A New Pentecost?* when he was still Patriarch of Venice. One very significant sentence in his warm and friendly letter of thanks summed up his reaction:

As far as the content is concerned, I have to confess that while reading it, I too felt obliged 'to reread with new eyes the texts of St Paul and of the Acts of the Apostles.' Your book was, and will remain for me, a precious guide in rereading the Acts.

The Renewal lives by this rereading of the New Testament.

Notes

1. F.A. Sullivan, 'The Pentecostal Movement,' offprint from *Gregorianum* (1972), vol. 53, fasc. 2, p. 249. See his book published under the title *Charisms and Charismatic Renewal* (Ann Arbor, Michigan: Servant Books, 1982).
2. R. Quedebaux, *The New Charismatics* (New York: Doubleday, 1976), p. 2.

+   +   +

Prayer

Let us express, in a prayer of thanksgiving, all our gratitude to the Lord for his Spirit's action in the Church throughout the ages:

LORD GOD, THE CREATION OF MAN WAS A WONDERFUL WORK; HIS REDEMPTION IS STILL MORE WONDERFUL. MAY WE PERSEVERE IN RIGHT REASON AGAINST ALL THAT ENTICES TO SIN AND SO ATTAIN TO EVERLASTING JOY.

Prayer of the Easter Vigil

+   +   +

Questions for reflection and discussion

1. The term 'charismatic' is ambiguous: each Christian is 'charismatic' by virtue of his Baptism. Clarify this term as applied to the 'Renewal in the Spirit' in the contemporary historical sense (no. 33).

2. What is central to the Renewal and what is peripheral to it? (no. 34).

3. Why did Jesus send the Holy Spirit to his disciples? (nos. 34 and 35).

4. Show, with reference to the Acts of the Apostles, that the Holy Spirit came to satisfy the vital needs of the Christian community (no. 35).

VII

The Renewal and a Deeper Sense of Evil

1. The Holy Spirit awakens us to the malevolence of Evil

36. The grace of the Renewal is not only a new religious experience, a keener appreciation of the gifts and charisms with which the Spirit upbuilds the ecclesial community: it embraces everything that is the work of the Spirit. Hence its action is felt not only in the luminous and positive aspects of the Christian life. Through the gift of understanding, it also sensitizes Christians to the reality of the world of darkness, the world which the Spirit rejects. It is giving them a new awareness of the reality of the Adversary, the Enemy of God's Kingdom.

A mysterious passage in St John's Gospel tells us that 'when the Spirit comes, he will confute the world regarding sin and righteousness and judgement' (John 16:8).

It is not easy to interpret this passage, but its general meaning is clear: the Holy Spirit reveals Christ—this is his direct mission—but in so doing he inevitably helps us to discover everything that is opposed to Christ, everything that pertains to the Antichrist.

So, according to Scripture, the Holy Spirit will reveal the world's iniquity and its condemnation. He will give the Christian a deeper awareness of the seriousness of sin and the omnipresence of evil. And he will also help the Christian to value the defeat of the Prince of this world—his self-defeat—

as a result of Jesus' Death and Resurrection.

One cannot love good without hating, not the sinner, but sin and evil. The Holy Spirit gives those who open themselves to him a sharper perception which enables them to see, to denounce and to fight against everything in the world that is a negation of God.

He not only reveals the depths of God but also fathoms the depths of man, urging him to react against the ravages of evil and sin, both personal and social.

37. Today we are becoming increasingly aware that sin is not only personal but also penetrates, on a much wider scale, our structures and social tensions.

Racial or partisan hatred, class selfishness, violence and terrorism, moral permissiveness and commercial exploitation, hypocrisy and lies—all these warp even the best of our human institutions. The Spirit gives us a keener insight into the deep causes of the disorder that cripples us as human beings. He helps us to perceive that the evil which disables us does not primarily lie in institutions or things, but in ourselves, in our will, in our soul. 'In itself the atom bomb is not dangerous,' says Denis de Rougemont, 'but what *is* dangerous is man.' To which I would add: 'What is dangerous is sin in man.' And whenever we speak of sin, we are venturing into a realm where the Spirit of Evil exerts his influence.

We need the penetrating light of the Holy Spirit to understand the full seriousness of evil and to acknowledge that we are sinners. Chesterton's definition of saintliness is appropriate here: 'A saint is a man who knows that he is a sinner.' Others do not know it or do not want to know it.

2. The Holy Spirit awakens us to the necessity of spiritual combat

38. It is therefore quite normal for the Holy Spirit to sharpen our perception of the dark background against which men play out their destiny. He puts us on the watch, ready for combat. In a book entitled *Concerning Spiritual Gifts,* the Protestant writer Donald Gee stresses this logic of the Holy Spirit:

> To the individual believer baptized in the Holy Ghost, and to the assembly experiencing the operation of spiritual gifts, the whole spiritual world becomes very real. It must inevitably follow that an increasing opening of the eyes to the reality of satanic power, will accompany a gracious granting of increasing spiritual visions to perceive the things of God.
>
> Happy is the believer, and happy the assembly, that meet these enlarged spiritual sensibilities in an attitude of watchfulness, but also of a supreme faith that God will always guard the Church purchased by his own blood, and finally defeat even the subtlest attacks of the great enemy.[1]

Note

1. Donald Gee, *Concerning Spiritual Gifts* (Springfield, Missouri: Gospel Publishing House, 1972), p. 60.

Prayer

Alerted by the Holy Spirit to the malevolence of sin, let us turn to the Lord:

GOD OUR FATHER, TEACH US TO FIND NEW LIFE THROUGH PENANCE, SO THAT OUR SOULS MAY BE HEALED. KEEP US FROM SIN, AND HELP US TO LIVE BY YOUR COMMANDMENT OF LOVE.

Prayer for Monday in the Second Week of Lent

+   +   +

Questions for reflection and discussion

1. 'The Holy Spirit will confute the world regarding sin, righteousness and judgement.' How is the Renewal opening our eyes to the malevolence of sin?

2. What does spiritual 'combat' mean? Are we aware of its implications?

3. The more a Christian conscience matures, the more it becomes aware of its weakness. Comment on Chesterton's saying (no. 37).

4. Note in the lives of past and present saints examples of this sense of humility before God.

VIII

The Renewal and
the Demonology Underlying
the Practice of Deliverance

39. Before studying how the ministry of 'deliverance from the Devil or devils' is practiced in the Renewal, we should consider what kind of demonology underlies this practice and note its doctrinal weakness. For here we are dealing with a contagious phenomenon which must hold our attention.

Historically, the Catholic Renewal was born in the United States, in a religious context where the fundamentalist reading of Scripture has played, and continues to play, an influential role.

At first, many Catholics in the Renewal discovered the practice of deliverance among Christians of other traditions, many of whom were members of the Pentecostal or Free Churches. As a result, the books they read at the time—and are still reading—mainly stem from those circles.

All this has given rise to a profuse literature on the Devil and his acolytes, his strategy, his maneuvres, and so on.

In the Catholic Church this field had lain fallow for quite a while and our own pastoral practice gave us few guidelines adapted to our time. We have to admit that on our side there was little guidance in this sphere, and it is not the fault of the members of the Renewal since they were not given up-to-date, authoritative directives when they most needed them.

This explains the osmosis that took place and the contagious effect of the exuberant, overconfident literature which invaded us, although it was alien to Catholic thinking. The excesses we are witnessing today in the sphere of demonology initially stem from that situation; but it must be admitted that some Catholic popularizers have helped to aggravate it.

It is not my intention here to draw up a detailed list of these excesses or to name those authors who have spread confusion in this field, for their good faith and pastoral concern are obvious and the extenuating circumstances are genuine.

But I would like to point out a series of assertions whose gratuitousness and lack of restraint are manifest. They are to be found in countless books, brochures and cassettes, some of which are circulated 'for private use,' although they are publicly on sale.

The immoderate demonism which I am about to describe does not, fortunately, affect all countries in the same degree, but there is so much widespread evidence of it that it has to be taken into account.

1. In non-Catholic circles

40. First let us note some typical exaggerations found in non-Catholic writings. They are particularly flagrant in the works of authors who attribute most, if not all, physical and psychiatric illnesses to demonic influences.

Demons and illnesses

One of these 'Masters of Demonology' calmly includes among the maladies which, in his view, are sometimes of demonic origin: insomnia, epilepsy, fits, cramps, migraine, asthma, sinusitis, tumours, ulcers, coronary thrombosis, arthritis, paralysis, deafness, dumbness and blindness.

The expulsion of demons

In his desire for accuracy, he even tells us how the demons depart from the afflicted person:

—the demon of fear usually departs with a kind of hysterical sob;
—the demon of falsehood and hatred gives a loud roar;
—the demon of nicotine leaves with a cough or a hiccup.

Specific features of demons

41. We also learn that each demon has a name which he acknowledges. These names include:
—Fear, Hatred, Falsehood, Doubt, Envy, Jealousy, Confusion, Perversity, Schizophrenia, Death, Suicide, Adultery, Mockery, Blasphemy and Witchcraft.

Demons and their numbers

Another book in the same vein provides a list of 323 types of demons and claims that the list is by no means exhaustive. It also tells us that schizophrenia is due to a complex of 15 (or more) devils, accompanied by inferior demons. A whole chapter of this book is devoted to a classification of the demons, who are listed in a 3-page summary table divided into 53 columns.

Demons and their organization

A manual of pastoral guidelines, which has many readers and followers, informs us that:
—Satan's army is a highly disciplined organization, comparable to the United States Army, with its own hierarchy consisting of a Commander-in-Chief, generals, colonels, majors, captains, lieutenants, etc.
—The soldiers of this diabolic army are assigned specific fields of action, such as a particular nation or city.

Demons and spiritual combat

We are advised to give battle to the demons and not merely to pray, for 'God has already answered our prayer by giving us authority and power over the Evil One.' It is up to us to exercise that power: 'Instead of praying to Heaven for what we have already received, let us start exercising those powers of deliverance which have already been conferred upon us.'

Demons and children

Deliverance, we are told, must also be ministered to children. A whole chapter is devoted to this subject: since there is good evidence that evil spirits are capable of invading a foetus or infants, it is obvious, we are told, that they too must be delivered. Demons who have taken possession of little children can be expelled, as they can from elderly people. As in other cases of deliverance, the expulsion will be manifested through the nostrils or the mouth.

2. In Catholic circles

In the literature of Catholic origin I would cite as examples a few assertions which are, to say the least, perplexing.

Agglomerated evil spirits

We are informed that the demons band together in groups and that among them the leading spirits can assume the voice of a human being, this being observed in at least one case out of ten.

Also that if two dominating spirits have come to reside in the same person, they fight against each other in order to obtain complete control of the person: this very battle is likely to engender mental disturbances. If voices are heard, this is a sign that the battle is taking place.

These same Catholic exponents quote as a particularly reliable authority an author who claims that 'evil spirits work together in groups of eight'!

Checked demons

Next we learn that sometimes the evil spirits are held in check and imprisoned together. The afflicted person's own unyielding nature—for example, his refusal to forgive—often provokes this phenomenon.

The stronger spirits, it seems, try to imprison the weaker ones. If, for example, a demon 'of revenge,' imprisoned by another evil spirit, is detected and cannot be expelled, one can often avoid him by circumventing him.

Strategy of the inferior demons

We are told that one must carefully diagnose the nature of the spirits and discern the dominating ones among them.

The inferior spirits are under the ascendancy of the dominating ones and sacrifice themselves in order to camouflage their masters.

How the demons depart

We are also informed that, though in the past demons left through a fit of coughing, nowadays they more frequently leave through a yawn. The exorcist's own yawns can hasten the process.

Objects and animals

It seems that mirrors and small ornaments from the Orient can lay themselves open to occult influences and in many cases should be banished from the home.

We even learn that a cat underwent a complete personality change after being invaded by a host of evil spirits.

The evil spirits can take over the exorcist

It is said that, because of the physical contact involved when the exorcist lays hands on the afflicted person, there is a serious risk of contagion. Should this happen, the team assisting the exorcist must immediately pray for his deliverance. And as if this were not enough, here are a few more examples:

—A popular preacher encourages the afflicted to vomit as a help in the expelling of demons.

—Another advises Christians to devote a few moments each day to the expulsion of their demons, as an integral part of the spiritual life.

A well-known ecclesiastical figure, whose stencilled writings, translated into several languages, are currently circulated and spreading much confusion, writes:

'Envisaging a possible victory, it is important to evaluate the strength of the evil spirits.
   This means that one must know:
   —who they are,
   —and the frequency with which they get up to their tricks;
   —then one must examine their strength: are they solid, robust, heavy?
   —And one must even take their size into consideration.
It took me two years to deliver a 16-year-old girl, and ultimately to cast out 25 demons from her.'

In the ministry of deliverance, practitioners are advised to discover the enemy's identity and to address him by name. The demon might send the afflicted person into convulsions or a trance, or torture him in various ways, but as long as he is not identified, he believes that the prayers are not directed against him. Consequently, the ministers are advised to ask the following questions:
1. Who are you?
2. How many are you?
3. How long have you dwelt in this person?
4. Where exactly do you dwell in him?
5. What illness have you caused in him?
In so doing, they must invoke the authority of Jesus' name with perseverance: 'I command you, in the name of Jesus, to speak and to reveal your names.' In some cases, they can only move the tongue of the afflicted person, who murmurs a few words. But the exorcist must persevere and force the devil to speak distinctly.
   The exorcist is advised to gaze intently three times into the afflicted person's eyes, and order him to return the gaze three times with equal intensity. The third time, the exorcist orders

him to close his eyes and to fall asleep; then having signed the sleeping subject with the sign of the Cross, he speaks to his soul.

The reader may ask: What is the point of publicizing such extravagancies, which can only harm the Renewal, provide a weapon for its critics, and create the impression that these excesses are standard practice in the Catholic Charismatic Renewal generally?

First, I must stress that, in fact, very many groups and communities throughout the world would not approve of the beliefs and practices I have just described and are therefore immune from these errors.

But since I believe in road safety, I consider that I am rendering the Renewal a service in pointing out the precipices that beset its path.

Then again I must point out that the contagion discussed in this chapter is insidious, and that to be forewarned is to be forearmed. And lastly I would emphasize that the Renewal can only gain in credibility if it takes the first step and denounces such a demonology. In this way, it will valorize the great spiritual richness which is inherent in it, and give us a more realistic grasp of the presence of the Powers of Evil and of the necessity of a truly spiritual combat.

Prayer

In unison with the whole Church, let us pray that the Lord may preserve us from the Powers of Evil and guide us in our spiritual battle:

GOD OUR FATHER, BY THE WATERS OF BAPTISM YOU GIVE NEW LIFE TO THE FAITHFUL. MAY WE NOT SUCCUMB TO THE INFLUENCE OF EVIL BUT REMAIN TRUE TO YOUR GIFT OF LIFE.

Prayer for Saturday in the Third Week of Easter

+   +   +

Questions for reflection and discussion

1. Compare the statements cited in this chapter with the Church's reserved attitude (nos. 4, 5, 24 and 25).

2. Why note and evaluate these excesses? Might we not detract from the credibility of the Renewal by giving them prominence? Analyse the answer to this objection (no. 41).

3. Have you noted other examples in the literature circulating in 'charismatic' circles or elsewhere?

4. How can we react concretely against the infiltration of a demonology that is alien to the mind of the Church as expressed today by her Magisterium?

IX

The Practice of 'Deliverance' in Catholic Circles

42. So far we have been examining our subject from the doctrinal standpoint. Let us now consider how this ministry of 'deliverance' (an understatement meaning, in fact, the act of exorcism) is practiced in Catholic circles.

1. What does 'exorcism' mean?

Our first step must be to look for a reliable definition of the word 'exorcism.' The *Dictionnaire de Théologie Catholique* defines it as follows:

> In the strict sense, exorcism is an adjuration addressed to the devil in order to force him to vacate a place, to abandon a situation, or to release a person whom he holds more or less in his power. The adjuration is made either in the form of a command given directly to the devil, but in the name of God or Jesus Christ, or in the form of a supplicatory invocation, addressed to God and to Our Lord, entreating them to order the devil to depart or to ensure that the order is executed.

One notes that this definition includes two different types of adjuration.

In the second type of adjuration the exorcist speaks directly and solely to God, entreating him to effect the deliverance himself. This is a supplication, a deprecatory prayer, addressed to God.

The first type of adjuration, on the other hand, is a command given directly, in the name of the Lord, to the Devil (or devils), who is ordered to free his victim. It is a direct command, a dialogue in which the exorcist will often attempt to force the Devil to reveal his identity and speciality. Sometimes this summons is called 'imprecatory prayer,' to distinguish it from 'deprecatory prayer,' but strictly speaking a Christian directs his prayer to God alone and never to the Devil.

Let us examine this first type of adjuration, for it poses some delicate problems which are in urgent need of a solution.

2. Description of the practice of 'deliverance'

43. How does a typical deliverance session unfold?

The following description is based on my personal memories and numerous testimonies. Naturally, there are variations depending on persons, cases and countries; but, basically, the practice retains a common structure and unfolds as follows:

First, let us look at the person 'to be delivered.'

This person has asked for 'deliverance,' either spontaneously or because it was suggested to him. And suggestion is such a potent process that quite often a real epidemic of deliverance sessions suddenly occurs, due to some particularly persuasive propagandist.

I have noticed that in some circles a prayer session for 'deliverance' is offered as if it were an indispensable rite for anyone desiring to live fully as a Christian. I have also observed that these 'deliverances' are rather frequently repeated, and not achieved once and for all.

One even meets the occasional prayer group or charismatic community where it is held that each future member must undergo one or several 'deliverances from evil spirits' (the terminology varies) as a kind of obligatory ritual introduction to 'baptism in the Spirit.'

The person to be delivered may fall either into the category of normal cases or into that of acute cases. In the latter instance, he believes himself to be the victim of uncontrollable oppressive forces, independent of his will and sometimes giving rise to strange phenomena. In all this, unconscious suggestion obviously plays an important role.

In the more usual and unspectacular cases, the person to be delivered is presumed to be bound by a diabolic influence, by one or several different types of evil spirits. He has allowed this or that evil tendency to enter him and will be asked to recognize it and denounce it. These tendencies have led to compulsions considered uncontrollable, such as alcoholism, drug addiction, sexual excesses, masturbation, kleptomania, and so on. In these circumstances the group will endeavour to liberate the afflicted person from the evil spirits that are enslaving him, to break the bonds that are impeding his freedom.

This direct summons to the Devil is given in the name of the Lord, and in a spirit of brotherly compassion and deep faith. But the exorcist does not address God alone; he directly adjures and commands the evil spirits to release their hold on the victim and to depart from him.

44. The deliverance is ministered in stages:
—The first, a preparatory stage, is devoted to prayer, generally offered by the whole group, and to the discernment of the case: the nature and cause of the affliction, the length of time it is likely to require, the follow-up, etc.

—The second stage consists of the actual 'prayer of deliverance,' which includes:
1. An initial prayer of praise and petition: the group prays that God may protect all present, and more particularly the exorcists who are exposing themselves to the attacks of the Evil One.
2. A prayer that the evil spirits may be 'bound' and thus lose their virulence in the victim.
3. An attempt, by means of questions and commands, to

discover the names and identities of the demons presumed responsible for the affliction, so that once they are identified, they may be more effectively driven out, one by one.
4. The prayer of the afflicted subject, who is asked to renounce, personally and voluntarily, the sin or sins underlying the specific demonic action which is binding and oppressing him.

The evil spirits, previously identified by name, are then commanded to depart from the oppressed person without harming anyone in the room, and to go where the Lord wills.

—The third and final stage: prayers of thanksgiving are offered by all present; then the team decides about the follow-up and whether a convalescence period is necessary.

Within this common framework the techniques may vary. Some practitioners believe that the exorcist should look deeply into the afflicted person's eyes to impress the indwelling demon(s); while others maintain that deliverance should be ministered with closed eyes. Some raise their voice to command the demons with greater force and authority. Others, on the contrary, assert that only a gently modulated voice is needed, since they are no longer acting by their own power, but in the Lord's name. In Catholic circles a crucifix, blessed salt or holy water are used.

Sometimes the person to be delivered is strongly encouraged to retch, since it appears that retching helps to cast out the demons. During a congress in Florida, I myself heard a woman testify that she had been 'delivered' after spewing fifteen demons.

In some rare cases these sessions can extend over several weeks or months. At a recent congress in the United States, a dozen priests proceeded to make adjurations of the kind described above for twelve hours on end, throughout the night, without achieving a definite result.

I am going into these details to help the reader visualize what happens in cases that are probably extreme but certainly revealing.

3. What is the precise meaning of the term 'deliverance?'

45. Those who exercise the 'ministry of deliverance' generally deny that they are practicing exorcism. They know that, strictly speaking, exorcism is practiced only in cases of possession presumed to be of a diabolic nature, and that this mandated practice, known as solemn exorcism, is reserved to the bishop or his delegate. Since they do not wish to give the impression that they are trespassing on forbidden ground, they adopt some other term with a more neutral connotation. Hence they speak of 'deliverance' sessions, 'liberation,' 'prayer of welcome,' 'special prayer,' 'prayer of compassion', 'intercessory prayer,' etc.

Why is their vocabulary so prudent? After all, no one doubts their charity and good faith. But various factors might explain the use of this vague and unassuming terminology. The more neutral and generally acceptable title may be used:

—either to avoid scaring away the persons they wish to help;

—or to avoid attracting the attention of the official ecclesiastical authorities, who might well be worried about this proliferation of deliverance sessions and regard them as unauthorized, 'contraband' exorcisms;

—or simply to discourage unhealthy curiosity or unbalanced enthusiasm. This would also explain the relative absence of publicity surrounding the practice of deliverance.

But whatever may be the reasons for discretion or secrecy, the fact remains that a great many 'deliverance' sessions or meetings are taking place—sometimes as a fringe activity of a congress or prayer evening, and at other times (as I said earlier) as the preliminary rite imposed on or strongly suggested to the person desiring to receive 'baptism in the Spirit' or to join a community.

This penumbra could very easily introduce into the Church a pastoral practice which could degenerate into esoterism. This would be quite alien to the Church, which does not have two separate teachings or ways of acting, one for the initiated and another for the rank and file.

4. *An ill-defined frontier*

46. Since 'deliverance' is exercised without a mandate and by way of direct exorcism, it poses a frontier problem which has to be clarified and solved. At first sight, the demarcation line seems clear: exorcism is reserved exclusively to the bishop or his delegate, when cases of presumed demoniacal possession arise. But since no provision has been made for the treatment of cases which do not come directly under this heading, the whole area is open to all and sundry.

Cases of genuine possession, which only the bishop or his delegate may deal with, are rare. But everything that falls short of possession in the strict sense remains a blurred, ill-defined area where confusion and ambiguity prevail. The complexity of the very vocabulary used to designate deliverance does not help to clarify matters: there is no commonly accepted terminology and very varied phenomena are classified under the same headings. Moreover, this whole domain does not easily lend itself to verbal definition.

How are total demoniacal possessions distinguished from partial ones, and what do such distinctions really mean? Are we dealing with an influence operating within or outside the afflicted subject? And how should we define the currently used terms: infestation, obsession, oppression, temptation, etc.?

All these problems need to be clarified in order to prevent Christians from venturing recklessly into the 'mystery of iniquity,' on their own authority, on the fringe of the Church and more or less without her knowledge.

In Part Three I offer some practical suggestions for dealing with this delicate matter.

Prayer

With the whole Church, let us ask the Father to grant us the true freedom of the children of God:

GOD OUR FATHER, YOU LOVED THE WORLD SO MUCH THAT YOU GAVE YOUR ONLY SON TO FREE US FROM THE ANCIENT POWER OF SIN AND DEATH. HELP US WHO WAIT FOR HIS COMING, AND LEAD US TO TRUE LIBERTY.

Prayer for Saturday in the First Week of Advent

+   +   +

Questions for reflection and discussion

1. In the 'definition of exorcism' (no. 42) two aspects of the official practice must be carefully distinguished. No. 42 is a key passage in the present study and calls for a meticulous analysis. Why?

2. The prayer of 'deliverance from Evil' is addressed to God and taught by Jesus himself. Analyse the meaning of the final petition in the Lord's Prayer: 'deliver us from evil' (with or without a capital 'E').

3. Why does the secrecy surrounding the word 'deliverance' and the practice it implies present such a serious danger?

4. Note the verbal ambiguities and the vagueness of the ill-defined frontier between 'possession' and the perverse influence which 'falls short of possession' (no. 46).

X

The Renewal and the Casting Out of Demons: Theological Observations

47. If the Catholic Church clearly affirms the existence and influence of the Powers of Evil, her systematic theology nonetheless remains very guarded on this subject. If ever there was a domain that must be approached very soberly, as St Paul advises, this is surely the one. We cannot even begin to describe the Devil except indirectly, by metaphors and the like. His strength lies in the very disguises he assumes; he is an illusionist by nature and the father of lies. Intrinsically and by definition, he is obscure. No one has ever seen the actual countenance of the Evil One, for he is a spiritual being, outside our reach, and known only as such through Revelation. And whatever those who recklessly venture into this minefield say to the contrary, his action is always deceitful and difficult to detect.

No man has ever seen the wind directly: we recognize its action by the leaves rustling on the trees and the dust it raises as it blows. In the same way, the Evil One does not divulge his true identity, his strategy, his intentions. Therefore it is all the more important to refrain from all exaggerations which could lead to obsessive psychosis. This would be the very negation of our Christian religion, which is Good News and the saving grace of Christ's victory.

In the final analysis, this domain has been entrusted to the

Magisterium, who alone has received from the Master the charism of ultimate discernment. To reject this teaching authority in favour of one's own personal experience would be incompatible with the Catholic faith. This point is important.

When reservations are made about the manner in which the expelling of demons is practiced, one comes up against the objections of those involved. They maintain that they have 'witnessed' the casting out of demons, and that there can be no doubt about the very great spiritual fruits of these deliverances.

1. Is experience the ultimate criterion of truth?

48. The argument drawn from 'personal experience' must be examined closely. What can it legitimately attest, and what are its limitations?

The practitioners of deliverance allege that healings have been obtained as a result of exorcisms; but here it would be wise to distinguish two aspects which are not necessarily identical and are often quite separate: 'healing' and 'the casting out of demons.'

A first question, then, is: How should we judge the healings adduced, even though they are sometimes spectacular? Can we deny their authority?

For my part, I have no valid reason for doubting that some of them are authentic, insofar as these very delicate matters can be judged at all. Jesus said: 'Wherever two or three are gathered in my name, I will be among them.' It is certainly in the name of Jesus, and by calling on him explicitly, that a group gathers to exercise a ministry of brotherly compassion. And God promised his own that healings would be accomplished in his name.

But can I go further than this and conclude that the healings in question are really due to the expulsion of one or several demons, commanded to depart from their victim? Everything hangs on this question: if a healing has taken place, it must certainly come from God, but has that healing been accomplished 'by casting out demons?'

What do we observe experimentally?

First, we observe the initial state of the victim of those compulsions and abnormalities. Then we observe that a given ritual, which retains a more or less identical structure everywhere, has been performed. And lastly, we note the final stage: the joy of the afflicted person, who has gained a feeling of liberation and peace.

But—and this is the crucial question—what allows us to conclude that the progress from the initial stage A to the final stage B is due to the expulsion of one or several demons who are thought to have held this person captive?

The conclusion goes well beyond the premises. The rules of logical reasoning do not allow us to conclude that, because the prayer and the deliverance are concomitant, there is a causal relation between them. *Cum hoc ergo propter hoc* is a good example of false inductive reasoning.

49. If the group clings to its interpretation by adducing the fruits of inner joy and peace which have resulted from the deliverance, I am obliged to say that here, too, prudence is essential. Can the fact that the effects are beneficial be a sufficient reason for attributing them to the casting out of the devil(s)?

On the purely natural plane, a sharing session between an oppressed person and a welcoming group can already in itself be liberating, and therefore fruitful and beneficial. The sympathetic care and attention with which the group listens to him is already a first step towards his healing. Apart from the divine grace conferred on these praying Christians, sharing has its own power to heal when it is done in a spirit of love.

Recovered inner peace and similar fruits can be observed in all kinds of sharing groups who, under diverse names, contribute to the liberation of their participants without there being any question of casting out devils.

So although no one could possibly deny that such valuable fruits as regained joy and peace are in fact obtained, to conclude that they are due to the subject's deliverance from demons is a rash presumption. It would be simplistic to conclude from the pragmatic observation that 'it works,' 'it is successful,' that the Devil has let go of his prey.

'The tree is judged by its fruits' is a valid saying provided that one examines all the fruits of the tree and establishes the connection between the fruit and the branch. But to do so in the present case, one would have to exclude all the other factors which could have contributed to the happy result, such as the brotherly compassion and sincere charity of the 'exorcists.'

These reflections have no other aim than to urge those engaged in deliverance not to draw premature conclusions which go beyond strict logic.

2. The Church is the only authorized interpreter

50. Since this study is addressed mainly to the faithful of the Catholic Church, I have to go even more deeply into the problem by pointing out the link between the necessary discernment and the very role of the teaching Church in her doctrinal and interpretative ministry of everything that pertains to the sphere of Revelation. Here we are in the realm of faith, and it is to the faith of the Church that I must adjust my own faith. 'Lord,' we say at each eucharistic celebration, 'look not on our sins but on the faith of your Church.'

A Christian or a group of Christians can never act in isolation; they can never be 'loners,' detached from their whole ecclesial community and the bishop who presides over it. We have to look to the faith of the Church, as lived and expressed through her teaching authority, and place our filial trust in her maternal wisdom. It is she who must guide us in an area which cannot be perceived or grasped by our reason alone.

The activities of the realm of darkness, the very existence and work of the evil spirits, elude our natural grasp—just as surely as do the existence and luminous role of the angels—and belong to the sphere of divine Revelation. God's Revelation was entrusted, by the Lord's positive will, to the apostles and their successors, established in the Holy Spirit as the interpreters who most faithfully interpret and preserve the Word of God illuminated by the Church's living Tradition.

Here it would be advisable to reread all the points I made in Chapter II concerning the Church as the interpreter of God's Word, for they express the traditional and unanimous doctrine of the Catholic Church. Since we believe in the Holy Spirit at work in the Church of Christ, let us acknowledge that in the matter of casting out demons we are not qualified to make authoritative decisions, and that experience itself must seek wisdom in the light of faith.

+   +   +

Prayer

Let us ask the Lord to transform our Christian life radically:

LORD, MAY THE MYSTERIES WE RECEIVE HEAL US AS ONLY YOU CAN HEAL US: MAY THEY REMOVE SIN FROM OUR HEARTS, AND MAKE US GROW STRONG UNDER YOUR CONSTANT PRO-TECTION.

Prayer for Wednesday in the Fifth Week of Lent

+   +   +

Questions for reflection and discussion

1. Why is 'experience' not the ultimate criterion which allows one to conclude that a casting out of demons has really taken place? (no. 48).

2. Why is it unwise to apply the scriptural saying, 'A tree is judged by its fruits,' to our topic? Discuss the meaning and limitations of this saying in the present context (no. 49).

3. Why is the hierarchical Church the only authority qualified to exercise the ultimate discernment in the matter of demonic activity and influences? (no. 50).

4. Note and discuss the 'liberating' effects of all acts of sharing, in human psychology and independently of any attempt to cast out demons (no. 49).

XI

The Renewal and the Casting Out of Demons: Psychological Observations

Let us pursue the analysis of deliverance sessions, but this time from a psychological viewpoint. On the psychological plane, too, we have to advance with extreme prudence, for we are dealing with the mind and the inward depths of the person seeking deliverance.

Here two particularly sensitive points must be noted:
—the first bears on the preliminary stage and the difficulty of making a correct diagnosis;
—the second concerns the psychological dangers to which both the 'exorcised' person and the 'exorcist' are exposed.

1. The difficulty of making a diagnosis

51. It is not easy to make a valid diagnosis, for how can one be certain that a demonic influence is at work? No one has direct evidence of it: since the demons are spiritual beings, they elude empirical observation and our intellectual categories.

So our diagnoses can only be presumptions. There is little need at this point to dwell on the variety of external manifestations which have been interpreted down the centuries, and according to diverse cultures, as signs of a diabolic presence.

But today we cannot disregard the findings of science, unless we wish to appear naive and over-credulous.

More than once I have noted in circles that practice deliverance excessively and unwisely an amazing ignorance of plain scientific facts.

A Christian group cannot disregard the findings of science. It has to retain its credibility; otherwise it may be rejected by the world at large.

Father de Tonquedec, S.J., a theologian of merit who, for many years, was an exorcist of the Paris diocese, wrote a book entitled *Les maladies nerveuses ou mentales et les manifestations diaboliques.* Though written some time ago, this work is still very topical and of importance to our subject, for it counsels those who immediately detect diabolic activity in strange forms of behaviour to think twice about their diagnosis.

De Tonquedec underlines certain features that are common to both genuine possession and nervous illnesses such as psychasthenia, hysteria and some forms of epilepsy.

Among other genuinely medical cases, he cites the condition known as split personality, leading to unusual manifestations quite uncharacteristic of the subject's normal behaviour: perverse and uncontrolled conduct, bestial and uncouth habits, etc. But all these manifestations are due to mental illness and, as such, have no diabolic significance.

Similarly, an hysterical subject who appears to behave as an instrument of Satan will exhibit a horror of religious objects and a taste for evil; at times he may be violently agitated and adopt foul language or shameless attitudes. [1]

Mental pathology knows a wide range of obsessions, including zoopathy—the belief that an animal is dwelling in one's abdomen.

The very special nature of these illnesses might lead some groups to presume that they are aberrations of a diabolic origin which can be remedied only by the exorcism practiced in deliverance.

No one would dream of resorting to exorcism in cases of cancer or leukemia, because the imagination is not stirred by the

symptoms of these diseases. The strange nature of the manifestations due to nervous illnesses should not allow anyone to
conclude there and then that they are due to demonic influences.

52. To disregard the scientific data amounts to ignoring the
close relation between grace and nature. St Thomas Aquinas
frequently stresses this relation when he says that grace does not
destroy nature, but completes and perfects it. Contrary to the
tendencies born of the Reformation, the Catholic Church does
not regard nature as being intrinsically vitiated or corrupted.

For our present purpose, I would add that the supernatural
charism of discernment, a gift of God, cannot dispense with the
critical human intelligence, which, like the whole of creation, is
also a gift of God: the charisms complete each other.

Consequently, we cannot adduce the gift of discernment as the
criterion which dispenses us from taking account of human
facts confirmed by psychiatry, and allows us to make a direct
appeal to the Holy Spirit without resorting to the discernment
of the Church. Generally, the discernment on which a deliverance team relies is that of the praying group and not of an
isolated individual. But even this collective discernment does
not suffice.

It is understandable that non-Catholic Christians may regard
that collective discernment as their ultimate criterion. But our
faith goes more deeply into the matter and helps us to recognize
the mystery of the Church, as the Master instituted her.

Christ desired his Church to be apostolic, and the apostolic
Church has continued down the ages through the succession of
bishops. It is on the bishops and the priests in communion with
them (or, as in the present case, mandated by them) that the
final judgement is incumbent, once the faithful have trustfully
and frankly informed them of the facts.

'Discernment' is yet another of those tricky words that
theology must clarify, if serious misunderstandings are to be
avoided.

2. *Psychological danger for the person to be 'delivered'*

53. Even if a group practices 'deliverance' wisely and discerningly, it must never overlook the psychological effects on the person 'to be delivered.' Usually, this person is convinced, or has been persuaded, that his ills are due to the influence of the Evil One.

Hence this person risks succumbing to a variety of complexes. In the first place, his own image of himself may become badly shaken through emotional shock, for he will consider himself the victim of fearful bonds and deadly influences which are partly or wholly independent of his responsibility and freedom.

To feel unaccountable for one's actions in this way is highly damaging, since the afflicted person's ability to co-operate in his healing risks being seriously diminished.

It is always reprehensible to foster an inferiority complex in a person and to diminish, in his own eyes, his capacity for action and reaction.

Consequently, it is important to analyse closely the reasons that prompt him to ask for deliverance. He may be tempted to look for a quick remedy, dispensing him from a more demanding self-discipline, or an easy way extrinsic to his real needs.

We must also take account of the collective contagion that may develop. From various countries of the world I have received testimonies that suddenly there is a great rush for deliverance and that a fashionable 'exorcist' may draw large crowds.

3. *Danger of domination on the part of the 'exorcist'*

54. But the most serious danger, in my view, lies in the hold that those administering deliverance may gain over the person who submits himself to exorcism.

That person is asked—sometimes in the course of many sessions—to reveal his most intimate disturbances. He is asked questions which attempt to lay bare his past, his mental or physical disorders, his remorse, his anguish, anxieties, hatred, and so on. The exorcist tries to identify the demon or demons whom he believes to be at the source of these disturbances and names them, one by one, with a view to driving them out.

Usually the person who submits himself to deliverance feels deeply grateful to his 'liberators' and is ready to follow their advice and suggestions for his future welfare almost blindly.

The danger of manipulating another person's mind in this way is very real, even when manipulation is not intended.

The Church, for her part, has always endeavoured to respect the person's privacy and freedom of conscience in her approved rules for the religious communities.

This time-honoured wisdom reminds us that there are certain barriers which must not be crossed, and that the person's freedom and responsibility must remain inviolable.

Note

1. J. de Tonquedec, *Les maladies nerveuses ou mentales et les manifestations diaboliques* (Paris, Beauchesne, 1938), pp. 23, 47, 82.

Prayer

The invisible world is shrouded in mystery, but the one thing we are certain of is that the Lord is present in the heart of our spiritual struggle. Let us join our prayer to the prayer of the Church:

> ALL-POWERFUL AND UNSEEN GOD, THE COMING OF YOUR LIGHT INTO OUR WORLD HAS MADE THE DARKNESS VANISH. TEACH US TO PROCLAIM THE BIRTH OF YOUR SON JESUS CHRIST, WHO LIVES AND REIGNS . . .

> *Prayer for the Fifth Day in the Octave of Christmas*

+   +   +

Questions for reflection and discussion

1. What is the role of the human sciences (particularly medicine and psychiatry) in the subject we have just examined? (no. 51).

2. What does the theological assertion 'grace does not destroy nature' mean in the present context? (no. 52).

3. By its very nature, the ministry of 'deliverance' involves the danger of violating the person's freedom of conscience and of gaining a hold on him. Analyse these dangers.

4. Why is the ministry of 'deliverance' in many cases a veritable practice of exorcism?

XII

The Necessary
Harmonization

55. The time has come to integrate Part Two of this study with Part One, that is to say, to integrate the Renewal into the heart of the Church and to show the necessary adjustments. We must avoid any hint of duality between the charismatic element and the institutional element of the one Church. In a recent Lenten conference at Notre Dame in Paris, Cardinal Etchegaray said: 'The Church is a mystery which one cannot stroll around as a sightseer; one has to enter it and plunge into it boldly, without reckoning the cost.'

This is what Part Three aims to discuss.

1. Two dimensions: only one Church

One cannot oppose 'hierarchy' to 'charism,' any more than one can oppose the work of the Incarnate Son to that of the Spirit who pursues it and actualizes it. The Church is one indivisible reality: her visible and sacramental institutional dimension is inseparable from her invisible dimension, to which the many and varied charisms of the Spirit belong.

Echoing the Church's Tradition, Karl Rahner, S.J., rightly points out that: 'The charismatic element belongs to the essence of the Church just as necessarily and permanently as the hierarchical ministry and the sacraments.'

The charismatic reality is an integral part of the Church's

very structure; it is not a kind of subsequent accretion, as if the institutional Church needed regularly a bit of 'extra soul' and an injection of dynamic power.

The Holy Spirit is already to be found at the very heart of the Church's ordained ministry.

When I became a deacon, the consecrating bishop said to me: 'Receive the Holy Spirit, so that he may be your strength and help you to resist the Devil and his temptations.' This formula may sound strange to modern ears. And yet . . .

When I was ordained priest, the bishop said to me: 'Receive the Holy Spirit. For those whose sins you forgive, they are forgiven.'

And, lastly, on the day of my episcopal consecration, the consecrating bishop said to me quite simply: 'Receive the Holy Spirit.'

So we deacons, priests and bishops are well and truly the inheritors of a same promise of Jesus. Together, we are the Anointed of the Spirit, but each according to his specific function which is complementary to the functions of the others.

The difference between the charisms of ordained ministers and those that are received and exercised in the spontaneity of the Spirit lies in the fact that, of themselves, the latter have a non-permanent character. The ministerial charisms which structure the Church exist so that the whole Church may blossom in the Spirit.

On the human plane, tensions may arise between these two aspects of the one Church, since both aspects are embodied in men and we all carry our treasures in fragile vessels. But a great step would be made in the Church's process of Renewal if we were all aware of our necessary and vital complementarity.

In this light, it would be unthinkable that a pastoral ministry of 'deliverance' could grow and teachings be given on the subject outside the control of the hierarchical Church and independently of it.

None of the faithful would question this principle, but it has to be embodied in practice. And this requires openness and trust on the part of the leaders of the Renewal, as well as a kindly welcome and a readiness to listen on the part of the ecclesial authorities whose mission it is to ensure this integration.

2. Present pastoral necessities

56. A serious pastoral problem is claiming our attention: it stems not only from the Renewal, which needs our guidance, but also from our contemporaries' obsession with everything that is directly or remotely connected with this area: satanism, occultism, clairvoyance, spiritualism, parapsychology . . .

Our task is to chart a safe course between an exaggerated demonism and a rationalism that dismisses the problems with scorn and complacency.

Here, then, are a few points which, I believe, should hold our joint attention.

(a) Necessity of an integral doctrinal teaching

At all levels of its activity, the teaching Church is duty-bound to remind Christians with clarity and precision—as Paul VI did— that the Devil's existence and insidious, multiform influence are not a myth, and that we have no right to adapt the Gospel to prevailing fashions by mutilating it.

This equally implies that Christians must be enlightened about the spiritual combat they have to wage, within themselves and around them, against the forces of evil. In order to fight the enemy, we must at least be able to recognize his favourite strongholds and battlefields. Here let us remember Pius X's wise remark that the power of evil thrives on the weakness of good men.

Our teaching must also be articulate about everything that concerns the concrete action of the Holy Spirit, and more particularly his charisms. Vatican II usefully and prophetically reminded us that the charisms did not belong to the primitive Church alone, but were a permanent part of our Christian heritage. And among the charisms, the one underlying the ministry of healing—especially inner healing—needs a delicate and indispensable doctrinal and pastoral discernment. Quite naturally, the 'ministry of deliverance' will find in that discernment the enlightenment it requires.

(b) Necessity of revising the criteria of the Roman rite

57. A second point, which is more limited but also very urgent, obliges us to take in hand as a pastoral duty the whole question of deliverance as practiced in the Renewal. It is essential for the good of the Church and for the credibility of the Renewal throughout the world to map out paths and to guarantee their safety with luminous road signs. The motorists are not the ones who establish the highway code, grant driving licenses or make the wearing of safety-belts compulsory. Within the Church that kind of service must be rendered by us bishops, who are responsible for the welfare of the Church.

From this point of view, it would be advisable to revise the criteria of the Roman Rite—which goes back to 1614—or at least those that enable us to recognize a case of demonic possession. Today these criteria are inadequate. They should be nuanced and studied in conjunction with natural parapsychological phenomena, such as telepathy, etc., which are in no sense diabolic and can even account for astonishing facts. [1]

No one can disregard what science has taught us in the area of psychology, parapsychology and extra-sensory perception. The exploration of the unconscious and the advances of medicine have brought to light aspects of human behaviour which were unknown to our ancestors. And it is highly probable that, in the not so distant future, other discoveries will enable the sciences of man and his behaviour to advance even further.

The demarcation line between the natural and the preternatural is becoming less and less rigid. This does not mean that it will disappear, but that it will be placed otherwise and elsewhere.

In the face of these strange phenomena, one can adopt three attitudes:

The *first* consists in reducing all of them to psychic, parapsychological or socio-cultural manifestations and in ruling out all other explanations. This is the most usual position of the scientific world today and, unfortunately, many Christians subscribe to it.

The *second* consists in assuming, on the basis of a few symptoms, that these phenomena are obvious manifestations of diabolic activity, and that they are discernible by a kind of immediate apprehension or inner revelation.

But a *third* attitude is possible: it consists in recognizing in the 'possessed' subjects cases of a psychic, parapsychological or psychopathological nature, while accepting the hypothesis that there, too, evil influences of a spiritual kind may play a role, concomitantly or separately, and contribute to the morbid behaviour.

The fact that a phenomenon can be explained according to our scientific categories does not allow us to rule out the possibility of an interpretation belonging to another order or level of reality.

We have to remind the scientist—if he is a Christian—that there are realities and dimensions which cannot be experimentally verified and that, furthermore, scientific objectivity does not allow us to dismiss other possible explanations in our interpretation of phenomena.

We have to tell the Christian who has not kept in touch with the findings and advances of science that the inquiring mind is also a gift of God and that naive credulity is not a virtue to be identified with faith.

Only a revision of the Roman Rite could help us to avoid premature judgements based on criteria that are no longer adequate for our time. This revision is all the more urgent as some groups who practice 'deliverance' adduce these criteria in order to multiply unduly the number of cases which, in their view, require their charitable intervention. This argument must be simply removed and made unavailable to them, since it allows them to call their practice orthodox and to regard anyone who advocates moderation and discretion as unorthodox and naturalistic.

*(c) The necessity of a new pastoral teaching
on the subject of exorcism*

58. A third urgent problem must be attended to: it is essential to work out a new pastoral teaching on what is in fact exorcism, regardless of the label attached to it by its unqualified practitioners. Whenever situations arise involving a direct summons, command or adjuration to the Devil or the devils with a view to their expulsion, the Church must lay down and present adequate rules which have to be obeyed. The code of canon law has reserved cases of possession to the bishop, but everything that 'falls short' of possession has remained vague and indeterminate. Furthermore, as I have already pointed out, there is a total lack of unity in the very vocabulary used in this area.

Since these points are in urgent need of clarification, it is essential to establish a consistent and commonly accepted terminology, and to draw a firm distinction between the *prayer* of deliverance and the *exorcism* of deliverance, effected by a *direct summons to the Devil.*

The *prayer of deliverance,* like every prayer, is addressed to God. The final petition of the *Our Father,* 'Deliver us from evil,' is the supreme prayer of deliverance. It is accessible to all and is part of our Christian heritage. We have to valorize this final petition by giving it all its dimension and its realism.

The *exorcism of deliverance,* on the other hand, presents a serious pastoral problem. The Church has laid down rules concerning diabolic possession by reserving such cases to the exclusive discernment of the bishop. But so far she has not drawn a clear demarcation line between the mandated practice and the forms of exorcism which are practiced in cases that 'fall short' of possession.

I know that in various countries bishops or episcopates have examined this question; some have even requested a moratorium until the line of conduct is clearly established. Understandably, even when the common guidelines are laid down, there may be variants due to different sociological contexts.

This would be the case when, for example, the problem is complicated by popular animistic beliefs or by the importance some people attribute to the spirits of the dead, witchcraft, and so on.

In the same way, the new Rite of Baptism provides a different form of renunciation for catechumens coming from a pagan society (Instruction 65, s2).

For the immediate future, given the urgent need to protect Christians from extravagances in this matter, it would be advisable, in my view, for the Church authorities to indicate clearly, at local or universal level, the limits that must not be exceeded in the practice of deliverance.

(d) *The episcopal reservation of exorcism in its relation to priests and laymen*

59. I believe that it is of the utmost importance to reserve to the bishop or his mandatary every form of exorcism that seeks to identify the Devil or the devils and to enter into dialogue with them by way of a direct summons, adjuration or command, with a view to their expulsion.

Hence the form of exorcism underlying the practice I have described in the previous chapters should, in my view, be reserved exclusively to the bishop's discernment and never be carried out without his consent.

This reservation is in the line of the Church's tradition, even where priests are concerned.

When a future priest was ordained as an 'exorcist'—in the days when the office of exorcist was a minor order—he was told that he received the power to exorcize, but that the exercise of this power remained reserved.

I would add that if the office of exorcist has disappeared as a minor order, there is nothing to prevent an episcopal conference from requesting Rome to restore it. I do not know if this is advisable, but it is at least a possibility which is deserving of study. If the conclusion is positive, then the office of exorcist could be made available to qualified laymen.

But whatever may be said of this point, it is very important, I believe, that the bishop, having been duly informed of the facts, should assume the ultimate responsibility and entrust this type of pastoral work to mandated priests and competent laymen.

Moreover, such a responsibility has already been assumed by bishops in various parts of the world. As an illustration of my point, in 1978 Cardinal Benelli, Archbishop of Florence, on realizing that the practice of exorcism was spreading and giving rise to serious abuses (in this case quite unconnected with the Renewal), publicly withdrew the powers of exorcism from all the priests who were exercising them in diverse forms, in order to reserve them solely to two priests mandated for this purpose.

I propose that not only presumed cases of diabolic possession be reserved to the bishop, in accordance with the Church's ancient law, but also all cases where a specifically demonic influence is suspected. In extending these reservations, it is by no means my intention to question the place and role of the layman in the Church. It is quite normal to make a distinction between a power inherent in every Christian and the exercise of that same power, which must depend on the ecclesial authorities.

Here we are not dealing with a theological problem concerning the role of the laity, but with the search for a prudential solution to the situations that arise.

Each Christian has the power to baptize, but the Church reserves the exercise of this power to cases of extreme necessity, and asks that the baptism be notified subsequently to the parish priest.

Each Christian who repents of his sins before God and turns to him in an act of perfect contrition, obtains forgiveness, but the priest remains the intermediary, and the penitent has to confess his sins by virtue of the priest's specific mission.

Every baptized man and woman who are united in marriage confer the sacrament of marriage on each other by mutual consent; yet, always for pastoral reasons, the Church establishes the rules of both the lawfulness and the validity of the marriage.

The priest, by his presence, ensures that this Christian marriage is incorporated into the mystery of the Church.

I am citing these few examples to illustrate how they are equally applicable to the question of 'exorcism.' Each baptized person has the radical power to exorcize by virtue of the Lord's promise and presence in him, but it is normal and salutary that the exercise of this power be regulated by the pastors of the Church according to the needs and requirements of an adequate pastoral practice.

In all this there is no clericalism, but simply respect for an order established by the Lord himself when he instituted the role and function of the pastors of the Church.

(e) Need for episcopal discernment

60. It would be unjust to accuse the Renewal of intruding into a 'reserved' domain since, in principle, its members agree not to venture into solemn exorcism; but, as I stressed earlier, the very demarcation line presents a problem.

It is essential to draw that line firmly: only the authority of the Church is in a position to do so for the faithful, who need her discernment, her directives and safeguards.

At the same time, the members of the Renewal must be assured that, in emphasizing the reality of the Forces of Evil, they are in the mainstream of the Church's Tradition.

But it is precisely because of a lack of contact and trust that, in many places, groups have introduced practices of deliverance, without benefiting from the Church's necessary directives and safeguards.

Despite good intentions, the extremely secretive or reticent nature of these practices have created an unhealthy atmosphere which cannot continue.

Fear that the bishop may forbid these practices without a preliminary hearing or adequate dialogue must be overcome. Let deliverance teams invite him to see for himself, or to send a deputy to check, how deliverance sessions are conducted.

I know that, when persons and concrete situations are

involved, dialogue with authority can sometimes be difficult on both sides. But the only solution is to accept, in a spirit of faith, the mystery of the Church founded on the apostles and their successors.

I have myself attended such sessions as a kindly and attentive observer, because I wished to grasp what was happening. I was moved by the compassion of the 'exorcists' and by their obvious love of the person they were seeking to deliver; but I felt uneasy on realizing that the dangers I have already pointed out in Chapters X and XI were not being avoided.

According to Catholic teaching, the Church is, in the first instance, the only interpreter authorized to discern the ways and interventions of the Spirit. When Paul, on his way to Damascus, encountered Jesus in a dazzling vision, the Lord did not give him direct instructions, but told him: 'Arise, go into the city and there you shall be told what you must do.' And this direction was the mission of Ananias.

Every believer in the Catholic Church, regardless of his personal vision or revelation, recognizes in Ananias the bishop of each local Church, in communion with the Bishop of Rome, the supreme guardian of unity.

The bishop has been defined as 'the man who has the charism of discerning charisms.' This obviously implies that he is duly informed of the facts which must contribute to his judgement. But if he did not play this vital role of discernment, illuminism would quickly dictate the law and the Renewal would degenerate into a sect. [2]

To conclude, let us consider a particular point. In order to justify the practice of direct exorcism, many Catholics adduce the authority of the 'Pope Leo XIII Exorcism' which, according to the circulated text, is permissible for both laymen and priests.

Since I wished to know the Church's official view on the subject of the Leo XIII exorcism, I asked the Sacred Congregation for the Doctrine of the Faith how that text should be interpreted. Shortly before his death, Cardinal Seper, in a letter of 18 November 1981, answered my query as follows:

The exorcism in question was incorporated into the *Rituale Romanum* in 1925 with the instruction: 'This exorcism can be recited by bishops, and also by priests authorized to do so by their bishops.'

In 1944 the Bishop of Citta della Pieve asked this Congregation whether it will licit for the faithful to recite the above-mentioned exorcism published during the pontificate of Leo XIII. The reply of the Holy Office was 'negative,' in view of the spirit of superstition to which the presentation of this exorcism has lent itself, and in view of the fact that the Church is accustomed to reserve the use of exorcism to its authorized ministers, as stipulated in C.I.C. 1151 and 1153.

I do not know how this type of exorcism ever became available to the faithful, as evidenced by the text circulating among them with imprimatur. This anomaly is yet another indication that here we have a general pastoral problem that needs to be thoroughly reexamined and clarified.

3. A call to the leaders of the Renewal

61. As a very sincere friend, I wish to say to the leaders of the Renewal: 'Do not be afraid to let yourselves be guided by your bishops; share your experiences, knowing that they are not the supreme criterion and that they need the light of the Church's faith and tradition. Make every effort to speak the language of the Church—our mother tongue—and to be in unison with her. The well-known saying *Sentire cum Ecclesia* expresses this intimate, mutual relationship. You must be recognized by your accent and not speak a foreign language, full of strange idioms.

Beware of living on the fringe of the Church. Do not let yourselves be led astray by esoteric or gnostic practices that unmandated leaders might advocate in the name of 'their experience.' Reread what I have said on our necessary and inevitable ignorance in matters pertaining to the Powers of Darkness, and mistrust over-peremptory assertions. The dialogue with your bishop will be all the more fruitful if you show a readiness to listen.

Your experience of prayer and healing, particularly inner healing, will be valuable, for it will help to reactualize a charism which was very familiar to the primitive Church and forms part of our Christian heritage.

Your task is both to give and to receive for the greater good of the Church.

4. A call to Church leaders

62. To my brother bishops and priests, I wish to say humbly but boldly: Let us open our hearts to the grace of the Renewal, grasping its meaning and spiritual wealth. Let us do this not only for ourselves but for our mission.

The defects of human beings must not hide from us the breadth and depth of the grace now offered to our freedom. This present action of the Spirit concerns numerous areas of our pastoral work. Let us not judge it from the outside; it can be understood only from within, that is, through a readiness to experience personally this new outpouring of the Spirit. I speak from personal experience.

Ask witnesses who are living this personal Pentecost to tell you what this outstanding grace of their second conversion means to them. You will find these witnesses in every land, in every social class: laymen, religious, priests and bishops.

I have tried to give my own witness to the Renewal in Chapter XII of my book *A New Pentecost?*. This title was formulated as a question because it is only through your warm and active support that the question-mark can disappear.

Our openness will make the necessary pastoral adjustments all the more effective, for the good of the Church and her saving work in today's world.

The Holy Spirit works in many ways, and no one can claim to have the monopoly of his action. But we have to recognize with Paul VI that the Renewal is 'an opportunity for the Church and the world,' and with John Paul II, who evaluates it after the experience of these last years that it is 'an opportunity being actualized before our eyes.'

Notes

1. For a discussion on this subject, see F.X. Maquart and J. de Tonquedec, 'L'Exorciste devant les manifestations diaboliques,' in *Satan,* pp. 328-50.
2. See the booklet *Reconnaître l'Esprit,* by Fathers Jacques Custeau and Robert Michel (Montreal, Service de Renouveau charismatique catholique, Ed. Bellarmin, 1974).

+ + +

Prayer

By inviting us to fast, the Church wishes to arm us for the spiritual combat. With her, we say:

LORD, WE PRAY FOR THE GRACE TO KEEP LENT FAITHFULLY. PROTECT US IN OUR STRUGGLE AGAINST EVIL. AS WE BEGIN THE DISCIPLINE OF LENT, MAKE THIS DAY HOLY BY OUR SELF-DENIAL.

Prayer for Ash Wednesday

+ + +

Questions for reflection and discussion

1. The whole Church is 'charismatic.' What does this assertion mean and what are its implications from the standpoint of the relations between the hierarchical and the charismatic aspects of the Church? (no. 55).

2. How do you conceive, in practice, the dialogue between the bishops and the leaders of the Renewal? (nos. 56, 57).

3. What reforms relating to our topic are desirable from the pastoral viewpoint and for the good of the whole Church? (nos. 59, 60, 61, 62).

4. What are the significance and the precise implications of the 'reservation to the bishop' advocated in this chapter? (no. 63).

XIII

Final Perspectives

A. The Paschal Perspective

1. Easter, at the heart of our faith

63. Christianity is indissolubly linked with the mystery of the paschal Resurrection.

We act out our present and future Christian existence against this fundamental reality of our faith; thus it is, quite literally, a matter of life and death.

The Christian is not someone who lives in an obsessive or pathological fear of the Devil or the devils; he believes in the Lord's Resurrection, in the triumph of life over death, of love over hatred, of truth over falsehood, of light over the darkness of night.

'We are a paschal people,' said John Paul II to the blacks of Harlem, 'and our song is "Alleluia"!'

The Christian does not see any of the stages of the redemptive mystery in isolation: he knows that Good Friday is the price of Easter, and that Easter introduces the dawn of Pentecost. He lives by this triple mystery of Good Friday, Easter and Pentecost, inseparably united.

The Christian is not expected to direct his attention to the Devil or the devils as if they were foremost in the Church's mind. St Theresa of Avila, with her magnificent common sense, used to say: 'I don't understand those fears that make us cry "the devil, the devil!" when we can say "God, God!"'

Christ's fight against the Adversary was radically victorious. From then on his Resurrection has dominated the horizon like an aurora borealis. Even if evil's hold on mankind has not yet been eliminated and vigilance remains essential, we know that the Kingdom of God is among us.

I believe in an infinitely tender Father; in Jesus our Saviour, who has already made us—in him—the inheritors of heaven; in the Spirit whose presence ensures for us 'a joy and peace that no man can take away from us.' My creed is poles apart from a religion of servile fear darkened by obsession with the powers of evil.

We cannot forget that Easter marks a victory over the Devil and evil; and this victory is so radical that we cannot simply transpose the pastoral methods of Jesus during his earthly life to his pastoral action today in the glory of his Resurrection.

Christ is acting and working now in a different way and notably through the sacraments, centred around the Eucharist, as the principal channels of grace. He is doing so on a worldwide scale, and no longer in the narrow context of Palestine and the customs of his time. Jesus' antidemonic action before the Resurrection cannot be simply transposed, as such, to the one he is pursuing today through his Spirit in the power of his Resurrection.

This reminder aims to avert the danger of a fundamentalist reading of Scripture and of any inadequate transference of the past to the present. In no sense does it fail to recognize the reality of Jesus' healings and casting out of devils: I am situating them in time and space, with the awareness that today we live under the sign of a victory already won and in the newness of the Spirit.

What lies at the heart of our faith is not demonology but Christ, in the power of the Spirit. When we lay undue emphasis on that realm of darkness, we are seriously endangering the balance of our Christianity and contradicting the Gospel, which is the Good News, the liberating message. The most cunning trap laid by the Evil One resides in his ability to draw attention to himself, and not to Jesus, the Saviour of the world.

We are, and will forever remain, the sons of Light.

2. The victorious Eucharist

64. When we concentrate all our attention on the devils, who have to be challenged and driven out by a direct summons, we risk forgetting that the Christian has other resources. Without restating here everything I said earlier on the Church as the sacrament of salvation, I would ask every Christian to remember that, in the struggle against the forces of darkness, he has at his disposal the power of prayer which is addressed to God and brings into play the Lord's paschal victory. In teaching us the *Our Father,* Jesus gave us the perfect model of the prayer that delivers us from all evil. It is the privileged prayer, which the Master taught his disciples for all times to come.

But we cannot forget either that a liberating power springs from the sacraments, and in particular from each eucharistic celebration, if we understand its value and significance. The whole of our liturgy's *Gloria in excelsis* could be commented on in this light. Each word of the *Gloria* reminds us of the finalities of the Eucharist, which is a prayer of worship, praise, supplication, thanksgiving, and by that very fact a victory over the powers of evil which are the negation of all those finalities. When we worship and glorify God, we are already freeing ourselves from the snares of evil, from all the idolatries that lie in wait for us and enslave us. When we fix our gaze on God, we are already turning away from darkness.

And when our prayer is embodied in a eucharistic celebration, this liberating power reaches its maximum intensity. It is not surprising that the demonological extravagances of the moment come mainly from circles unacquainted with the Eucharist.

Our fathers in the faith were well aware of this close link between worship and thanksgiving, on the one hand, and the confusion of the enemy, on the other. As early as the second

century, St Ignatius of Antioch wrote to the Ephesians: 'Do
your best, then, to meet more often to give thanks and glory to
God. When you meet frequently, the powers of Satan are
confounded, and in the face of your corporate faith his
maleficence crumbles.' (*Letter to the Ephesians,* nos. 13-18)

3. The victorious name of Jesus

65. This paschal awareness is manifested on each page of the
Acts of the Apostles. Already in the first miracle of healing
recorded in the Acts, Peter says to the lame man lying at the gate
of the Temple: 'I have neither silver nor gold, but I give you
what I have: in the name of Jesus Christ the Nazarene, get up
and walk!'

The very name of Jesus signifies victory. When the angel
appeared to Joseph in a dream, he told him that Mary would
bear a son and added: 'You must name him Jesus, for it is he
who will save his people from their sins.'

When we invoke his name, we are already protecting
ourselves against the onslaughts of evil, for we are resorting to
the very power of the Resurrection. 'Power has gone forth from
me,' said Jesus to the woman who touched the hem of his cloak:
a power of sovereignty, healing and courage also springs from
the very name of Jesus pronounced with faith.

Our ancestors had a veneration for this name. For my part, I
regret that the Litany of the Holy Name of Jesus—so rich in
meaning—has fallen into disuse in our Western Christianity.
But one notes with joy that the 'Jesus Prayer,' so familiar to the
Eastern Church, has found a new resonance in our midst. This
'prayer of the heart,' in which the sacred name of Jesus
coincides with the rhythm of our own heartbeats, makes us live
in a constant paschal climate and makes our whole person a
continuous profession of faith in the central truth of our creed
'that there is salvation in no one else, for there is no other name
under heaven given to men by which we must be saved' (Acts
4:12).

4. *Conversely*

66. Conversely, if we pushed the logic of the extremist demonology to its ultimate conclusion, we would have to attach so much importance to our antidemonic reactions that it would be difficult to know where to stop.

If the Devil is at the origin of our illnesses, our changes of mood, our weaknesses and aggression, our many and varied troubles, we would have to take the offensive at every moment of the day. And why not go further and devote a regular time each day (as some have actually suggested!) to prayers of deliverance or to a direct 'challenging' of the Devil? And all this would have to be taught in our catechism classes, translated into our pastoral work, woven into our religious constitutions. Exorcism sessions would have to be held before candidates could be admitted to our novitiates and scholasticates. And why not in our pastoral councils at all levels?

At this point I put a halt to these alarming considerations: they sufficiently prove the necessity of revising the 'theology' underlying the demonism we are denouncing. In no sense is that climate, that obsession, to be found in the spiritual life of the Church, and her liturgy speaks quite another language. Such an atmosphere is unbreathable in the Catholic Church, and such an esoteric teaching with its improper practices would turn our charismatic groups into groups living on the fringe of the great Church and cut off from her vivifying breath.

B. Full Ecclesial Perspectives

67. In the face of the Powers of Darkness, we can and must immerse ourselves in Christ's victory. But it is not only the victory of Christ Jesus, the Head of the Church: it is already shining forth now in the triumphant Church: the saints of heaven.

Vatican II has reminded us that here below we are a pilgrim Church, with all that this journey involves in terms of dangers, weariness, dullness. But at the same time it has underlined our solidarity with the triumphant Church, which is united with us in a mysterious, exalting way (*Lumen Gentium,* nos. 8 and 51).

It is heartening to know that in the struggle against the forces of Evil, we are not alone, but living in profound unity with the Church in heaven.

Thus we rediscover the great biblical vision which brings together, in the glory of heaven, Christ and all the redeemed who are united with him for ever. In him, through him, they are more than ever alive and close to us. In fact, they are the ones who are most supremely alive.

1. Mary and the saints

68. In an eminent and unique way, Mary is there as 'the eschatological image of the Church,' and with her the angels and the saints. The unique activity of the triumphant Church on our behalf is precisely its intercession until the fulfilment of salvation history. St Paul presents it as a 'combat' against the hostile powers and as intercession (1 Cor. 15:24-28; Rom. 8:34; and even more significantly Heb. 7:25; 9:24; 10:13-14). In his *Spiritual Exercises,* St Ignatius asks the retreatant to picture Christ and the heavenly court interceding on his behalf. There we have a full vision, which today we sometimes forget or diminish in our Christian behaviour.

The Church's Tradition and the piety of the faithful have never ceased to recognize Mary's role and place in this intercessory communion of saints and in its victorious opposition to evil.

The combat against the Spirit of Evil began when the world was created, through the radical enmity established by God between the woman and the serpent (Gen. 3:15). In this woman of Genesis, the Church has always recognized Mary, the new Eve, the mother of the living. Christians of all ages have had recourse to her protection.

United with her Son in the mystery of the Redemption, Mary

remains forever concerned with the fruitfulness of this redemption, as indeed with everything that hinders it.

Instinctively, the Christian feels that Mary is a powerful
protection against the spirits of evil and that, in profound
communion with her, he finds the strength to fight against
temptations and everything that threatens the life of Christ
Jesus in us. In communion of soul with Mary, and by
pronouncing with her lips and her heart 'the Name which is
above all other names, so that all beings in heaven, on earth and
in the underworld should bend the knee at the name of Jesus
(Phil. 2:10), the Christian brings Jesus Christ's victory into play
in a unique manner. For us faithful of the Church, spiritual
communion with Mary is a pledge of immunity and deliverance
in the spiritual combat we have to wage here below while
awaiting the final encounter in God's glory.

We recognize Mary in heaven as the Queen of the Saints and
the Angels.

⊙   *2. The angels*

69. Today's Christians must equally be reminded that here
below we live in communion with the angels of heaven. It is the
mission of the angels, too, to help us in the ongoing spiritual
combat. Any silence about their role unbalances the Church's
teaching on the fallen angels, and such an omission distorts the
total vision—a luminous vision for the Christian who believes,
with the Church, that the world of spirits is a living reality, and
that in it the angels play a mysterious role, ever close to us.

The Church teaches us this intimacy with the invisible world
of the angels and with St Michael, whom she considers their
leader. She invokes them in her liturgy with the words: 'Lord,
you have arranged the service of angels and men in a wonderful
harmony; grant in your mercy that those who always serve
before you in heaven may be the protectors of our life on earth'
(Prayer for the Feast of the Holy Archangels, 29 September).

The Church's Tradition sees in St Michael, the angel of light, the first adversary of Satan; it is he who defends the primacy of God: in Hebrew the name Michael means 'Who is like God.'

In former days we used to invoke him at the end of each eucharistic celebration:

> Holy Archangel Michael, defender in the hour of conflict, be our safeguard against the snares of the devil. May God restrain him, we humbly pray, and do thou, O prince of the heavenly host, by the power of God, thrust down to hell Satan and with him all the other wicked spirits who wander through the world for the ruin of souls.

How strengthening it is to know one's allies and to be able to count on their attentive support! Already in the seventeenth century, Bossuet would remind his contemporaries of this: 'You believe that you have dealings only with men, and all your thoughts are bent on satisfying them, as if the angels did not affect you. Christians, open your eyes to the truth: there is an invisible people—the angels—united with you by charity.'

This is a familiar idea. It recurs frequently in the patristic tradition, which saw in the guardian angels, to whose protection God has entrusted us, one of the concrete signs of Providence.

The world of the angels, so richly present in the tradition of the Eastern Churches, both Catholic and Orthodox, has to be integrated into our daily life: it illuminates with its all-embracing light the tenebrous world of the spirits to whom we will be exposed as long as we remain the pilgrim Church.

It would be highly desirable for the teaching given in the Renewal to lay stress on the luminous presence of the angels, both out of a concern for truth and in order to balance the too unilateral and emphatic statements that are sometimes made about the Powers of Darkness.

Prayer

With this prayer of the Church, let us ask the Lord that we may be true witnesses to the paschal mystery, the heart of our whole Christian life:

ALL-POWERFUL GOD, HELP US TO PROCLAIM THE POWER OF THE LORD'S RESURRECTION. MAY WE WHO ACCEPT THIS SIGN OF THE LOVE OF CHRIST COME TO SHARE THE ETERNAL LIFE HE REVEALS.

Prayer for Tuesday in the Second Week of Easter

✛   ✛   ✛

Questions for reflection and discussion

1. Easter is at the heart of our Christian religion: what consequences flow from our underlining of this fundamental truth in the face of the struggle against the Powers of Evil? (no. 63).

2. Why is it important for us to extend our ecclesial horizon to the dimensions of the triumphant Church? Do we read the lives and the writings of the saints? Have we maintained this communion with the Church and the saints of heaven? What does 'believing with the faith of the whole Church' mean? (no. 67).

3. What is the eminent place of Mary, the Mother of the Church, in the spiritual combat we have to wage against the Powers of Darkness?

4. The Church's liturgy makes numerous allusions to the

angels. Single out a few texts which can help today's Christians become aware, or to renew their awareness, of their active presence.

Conclusion

70. As I conclude these pages, I confess that I too feel challenged, realizing that in the course of my pastoral ministry I have not sufficiently stressed the reality of the Powers of Evil at work in our contemporary world, and the necessity of the spiritual combat we must all wage.

It is difficult to row against the tide and not to succumb to the spirit of the times. And all the more so as, in this delicate matter, we have to steer a safe course between Scylla and Charybdis, between underestimation and exaggeration: we have to assert with firmness that the Evil One does exist, yet profess a triumphant paschal faith; we have to make room for a ministry of deliverance without drifting into the very excesses we were obliged to denounce.

All this was, for me primarily, an opportunity for an examination of conscience, and an invitation to believe, with a living faith, in both the luminous realities of our faith and the mystery of iniquity, which is only too real in a world morally adrift. This, too, must be said, even at the risk of offending those who obstinately place their trust in the natural goodness of man and the myth of 'Progress.'

71. Turning to the faithful, whether or not they participate in the Renewal, I would like to wish them the grace to discover the mystery of the Church in ever greater depth. We are constantly tempted to reduce the Church, that is to say, to equate her with a more or less well-organized and up-to-date human sociological institution. And we do not immerse ourselves in her profound mystery which shows her to be the continuation of Jesus Christ's earthly mission.

It is in the Church that we must encounter the Holy Spirit,

and it is in her that he guides us according to the plan of God, who from the beginning desired a holy, apostolic Church. Today's apostles are the bishops, established by the Holy Spirit to lead the Christian people. To have good relations with them does not suffice; here we are not on the level of courtesy or diplomacy, but on the level of faith, and it is faith which must animate us and motivate filial and trustful obedience.

While awaiting directives, which I trust will be given soon, on the subject of 'deliverance,' it is also my fervent hope that the International Theological Commission will help to clear the way, to clarify a very loose vocabulary dependent on the whims of authors, and to draw a clear demarcation line that can guide our pastoral work.

And how can one fail to hope, too, that, in the future, books, brochures and cassettes which do not reflect the mind of the Church's living Magisterium will no longer be on sale at meetings and congresses of the Renewal; and also that the faithful will beware of any pragmatic outlook which too hastily concludes from beneficial effects ('it works') that it is legitimate to resort to a ministry of deliverance which must itself be duly accredited.

The Renewal is a precious grace which is offered to the Church and can powerfully contribute to the spiritual rebirth that the world so urgently needs. It must not isolate itself or live on the fringe of the Church. The sap rises all the better in the tree as the tree protects it against the fitfulness of nature by means of its very bark.

I have pointed out on the way certain pitfalls that Christians must avoid at all costs if they are not to succumb to the wiles of the Evil One, who insidiously seeks to capture their attention and thus to turn their gaze away from the luminous face of the Saviour.

This book will have achieved its aim if we adopt as our own the prayer of the Psalmist, with all its implications:

I seek the Lord, and he answers me
and frees me from all my fears.

Every face turned to him grows radiant
and is never ashamed.
(Ps. 34:4-5)